THE LA~~~~

CHATTERLEY

TRIAL

REVISITED

by David Holding

Published by
Scott Martin Productions, 2021

First published in Great Britain in 2021 by
Scott Martin Productions
10 Chester Place,
Adlington, Chorley, PR6 9RP
scottmartinproductions@gmail.com
www.scottmartinproductions.com

Electronic version and paperback versions available for purchase on Amazon.
Copyright (c) David Holding and Scott Martin Productions.

First edition 2021.

The right of David Holding to be identified as the author of this work has been asserted by him in accordance with the Copyright, Design and Patents Act 1988.

Acknowledgements

I am most grateful for the support and encouragement I have received during the preparation of this work. This includes the numerous helpful staff at the libraries and archives I have consulted, and my gratitude loses no sincerity in its generality. Whilst the *'Lady Chatterley'* trial has been the subject of numerous publications, academic papers and media articles; this work takes a multi-faceted approach to the case. It emphasises the literary, political, legal and social impact of Lawrence's novel. This approach, it is hoped, will provide readers with a 'holistic' overview of this important trial. The sources consulted in this work include archive material at both the National Archives and Bristol University library. The relevant law reports and records of Parliamentary Debates reported in Hansard have also been consulted. These have been supplemented by reference to two standard works which provide a verbatim account of the trial, namely CH Rolph and Sybille Bedford's accounts of the trial. In addition, selected press reports have also been used to reflect public perceptions of the trial.

No acknowledgement would be complete without expressing my sincere thanks and appreciation to my publisher, Lesley Atherton. Her total commitment and constant support of my work are boundless.

David Holding, 2021

Dr David Holding studied history at Manchester University before entering the teaching profession in the 1970s. He taught in both state and independent sectors. It was during this time that he continued historical research culminating in the award of both a Master's degree and Doctorate.

Having previously studied law, David gained a Master of Laws degree in Medical Law, which enabled him to transfer to teaching legal courses at university. Since retiring, David has concentrated his research and writing on various aspects of local history, legal trials, forensic science and medico-legal topics.

Also By David Holding

Murder in the Heather: The Winter Hill Murder of 1838

This book is a unique account of a brutal murder which occurred on the summit of Winter Hill in Lancashire in 1838. The account draws on both contemporary media reports and court transcripts and examines the events leading up to the killing of a 21-year-old packman. It details the proceedings of the trial of the only suspect in the case. The work concludes with a re-assessment of the case in the light of modern forensic investigation. The reader is invited to reach their own 'verdict' based on the evidence provided.

The Pendle Witch Trials of 1612

The book provides readers with a sequential overview of the famous chain of events which ultimately led to the execution of women accused of practising witchcraft in the county of Lancashire. It is presented as a chronological account of the famous trials at Lancaster Castle in 1612. The reader is introduced to all the evidence and interview transcripts that formed the major plank of the prosecution case in this book that will appeal to both the general reader and local historian.

The Dark Figure: Crime in Victorian Bolton

This book provides an absorbing overview of crime in the Lancashire town of Bolton over the period 1850 to 1890. It is primarily based on documentary survey and analysis of court and police records covering the period. It assesses changes in crime over time and asks whether these relate to economic, social or political changes taking place at the same time. The reader is left to reflect on whether crime in all its many forms, has actually changed over time.

Bleak Christmas: The Pretoria Colliery Disaster of 1910

This work charts the events of the Lancashire Pretoria Pit disaster in December 1910. It reflects on the devastation it left to many of the local communities whose main source of employment was coal. The main sources analysed are the Home Office Report into the disaster and the Report of the Inquest. The findings of these detailed legal reports are presented in a format that will supplement existing material on the event. The book will also provide a reference source for both local historians and the general interested reader.

Doctors in the Dock: The Trials of Doctors Harold Shipman, John Bodkin Adams and Buck Ruxton

This book takes the reader on a journey into the world of three medical doctors in England, each coming from a different social background but with one common thread going through their lives. They all stood trial for murder. In each of the cases, the reader is involved from the start and presented with all relevant evidence available to jurors in the case. The overall aim of this work is to invite readers to exercise their judgment in reaching a verdict.

Forensic Science Basics: Every Contact Leaves a Trace

Starting from the basic principle of forensic science, this work is an absorbing introductory study of the techniques familiar to us all from numerous trials, media reports and TV crime dramas. The book examines such aspects as the time of death, causes of death, weapons of crime and identification of offenders and much more. It provides essential reading for those who wish to gain a basic introduction to this fascinating area of science.

A Warning from History: The Influenza Pandemic of 1918

The 1918 Influenza Pandemic was one of the most deadly events in human history, and understanding the events and experience of 1918 is of great importance to pandemic preparation. This book aims to address questions concerning pandemic origin, features and causes, and to provide the reader with an appreciation of the 1918 pandemic and its implications for future pandemics. This work will cater to both the science-orientated and general reader in this crucial area of global and public health.

CONTENTS

Introduction

When Penguin Books released a new, unexpurgated edition of DH Lawrence's *Lady Chatterley's Lover* in 1960, they were charged with publishing obscene material. The *R v Penguin Books Limited* trial took place between the 20th of October and the 2nd of November 1960 in Court No 1 at the Old Bailey, London. This involved the judge, the jury, prosecution and defence counsel and 35 witnesses; all called to support Penguin's planned publication of an unexpurgated edition of Lawrence's final novel.

First published in Florence in 1928 and Paris in 1929, the novel had not been published in Britain and the USA for fear of prosecution. However, British readers did have legal access to an expurgated text from publishers, Heinemann, while uncensored editions were smuggled in from Europe. However, these were regularly confiscated by customs officials, with importers and retailers risking prosecution. One Soho bookseller was jailed for two months in 1955. When Penguin Books released a new unexpurgated edition in 1960, they were charged with publishing obscene material contrary to the new Obscene Publications Act of 1959.

The trial of October-November 1960, which ended with Penguin's acquittal, attracted considerable interest and has become one of the best-known episodes in modern British legal history. The trial has been viewed as the catalyst for changing post-war attitudes to social order and public decency, and as the starting point for a decade of conflict between champions of moralism and liberalism. The year 1959 saw the enactment of a new Obscene Publications Act which introduced a defence for publishers if they could show that a work was of '*literary merit*' and '*for the public good*'. The trial of Penguin Books was a

8

'test' case of this new law regarding obscenity.

The prosecution maintained that the book's 'pornographic' elements far outweighed any considerations of 'literary merit'.

The defence argued that the book's literary qualities and the author's status as a writer of significant standing should take precedence over 'prudish' notions of what constitutes obscenity.

The defence called 35 witnesses which included authors, academics, clergymen and MPs. Ironically, the prosecution called no witnesses.

This work follows the trial event over the six days in 1960, and introduces the reader to the trial process; the examinations-in-chief and cross-examinations of the witnesses, the opening and closing addresses by prosecution and defence counsel and the judge's summing-up to the jury at the conclusion of the trial. The final chapter takes a retrospective overview of the case and its impact on society.

Since prosecuting counsel chose to cross-examine only 14 of the 35 defence witnesses, ten of those witnesses have been chosen to represent a cross-section consensus, which supported the literary merits of the novel. Their testimonies are based on court transcripts of the trial, as are the prosecution and defence narratives. In this way, the reader is presented with the evidence available to the jury at the original trial. This will enable the reader to reach a considered assessment of the case.

Looking at this case in retrospect, it is clear that Penguin's victory had a lasting impact. For one thing, the government's jurisdiction over personal morality had weakened. Censorship was now being seen as an infringement of individual judgment and personal ethics. The beginning of the 1960s saw conservative attitudes beginning to take a back seat. Young people were moving away from the 'staid and proper' behaviour of their parents and grand-parents. Outlooks were changing. Even attitudes towards the trial itself were liberal; some newspaper editorials suggested the money spent on prosecuting a work of literature would have been better spent in the investigation of *actual* exploitive pornography. After reading this work, the reader is left to consider one important question; can 'certain' literature *truly* corrupt us, or does it just make for expensive court trials?

CHAPTER ONE

Early Beginnings

In 1857 Britain passed the first Obscene Publications Act which empowered magistrates to order the destruction of obscene books and authorise warrants to enable police to search premises. The sponsor of the Act, Lord Campbell assured the House of Lords that:

> "...*the measure was intended to apply exclusively to works written for the single purpose of corrupting the morals of youth, and of a nature calculated to shock the common feelings of decency in a well-regulated mind".*
> (Hansard, 3rd Series, H.C. Vol 146).

However, the task of defining 'obscenity' was the prerogative of the courts, and it was not until 1868 that a definition was provided.

In the case of *R v Hicklin* (1868. L.R. 3 QB, p 371) the trial judge, Chief Justice Cockburn, stated:

> "*I think the test of obscenity is this, whether the tendency of the matter charged as obscene, is to 'deprave and corrupt' those whose minds are open to such immoral influences, and into whose hands a publication of this sort may fall".*

Under the 1857 Act, the offence of 'obscene libel' covered almost any work which expressed sexual passions and could be successfully prosecuted. What has been referred to as the *Hicklin Test,* focused on the effect the book had on the most vulnerable in society, irrespective of whether they

11

were ever likely to read it. Consequently, even one passage of obscenity could render a novel to be condemned as 'obscene'. There was no defence available in respect of 'literary merit'.

Of particular relevance was the fact that the 1857 Act did not require the courts to consider the work as a 'whole'. As a result, prosecuting counsel were actively encouraged by some judges to select the 'highlights' or what have been termed *'purple passages'* from the book to quote them out of context to convince the jury of the 'obscene' character of the whole book. There was no decision concerning the relevance of the literary, scientific or educational values of the work as a defence.

To complicate things even further, judges refused to hear evidence from 'expert' witnesses on the work's values, so a defence of 'literary merit' could not be mounted. In addition, the position of the author was a difficult one because his books could be destroyed without him being a party to the legal proceedings for obscenity without his actual knowledge.

In 1923, the United Kingdom became a signatory to an international convention for the *'suppression of the circulation and trafficking in obscene publications'*. This resulted in an increase in prosecutions for obscenity in Britain. In particular, these prosecutions centred upon serious works of literature.

In 1928, the British Government applied for a destruction order for the novel, *"The Well of Loneliness"* by the acclaimed writer Radcliffe Hall. For the magistrates' court hearing of the case, the defence assembled forty expert witnesses in support of the book's publication. Despite this, the Bow Street magistrate hearing the case refused to admit the evidence of these witnesses as to the work's merits. The magistrate even announced to the court that it was he, and he alone, who would decide whether the work was obscene. Not surprisingly he did decide - and ordered the book's destruction.

However, during the following two decades, there appears to have been a gradual decrease in the number of prosecutions against works of literature, though in 1954 there was once again an unexpected revival of prosecutions against 'alleged' obscene novels. The publishers Hutchinson, Heinemann, Secker and Warburg, Werner and Arthur Barker, were all prosecuted for publishing obscene works.

It was as a result of this outburst of activity that the *Society of Authors* was prompted to establish a Committee with Sir Alan Herbert as its Chairman. This Committee produced a draft Bill for reforming the existing Obscene Publications Act of 1857. This Bill was first introduced into the House of Commons by Roy Jenkins MP under the 'Ten Minute Rule', but it did not progress any further at that stage. However, in 1955 and 1956 respectively, Mr Hugh Fraser MP and Lord Lambton MP made further attempts to launch this Bill. In March 1957, the Bill was eventually referred to a Commons Select Committee on its second reading in the House. The Select Committee reported back to the House in March 1958. The Bill then passed to the House of Lords in April 1959 for a second reading having passed the House of Commons with all-party support.

The proposed Obscene Publications Bill was a compromise between the Herbert Committee who considered that recent court decisions had seriously jeopardised literary freedom and the Home Office and police who wanted to strengthen the law concerning the sale of pornography. In agreeing to sponsor the Bill in the House of Lords, Lord Norman Birkett, the eminent barrister, hoped that the new Bill would provide for the protection of literature as well as strengthen the law against pornography.

Lord Birkett delivered a memorable speech to the

13

House of Lords on the 2nd June 1959:

"My Lords, it is enough for me to say
that it has been widely felt that, while it is
important that pornography should be struck at
with vigour, and everybody would support such
an action, we ought to be extremely careful not
to injure true literature. In my submission to
your Lordships, the freedom to write is a great
freedom; your English writer must be free and
permitted to depict the thoughts and feelings,
the customs, the prejudices and the weaknesses
which form the complexity of human
behaviour, the ideas which are current in all
sorts and conditions of men. He must be able to
set them down not only for his own generation
but, it may be, for the generations that are still
to come.

The promoters of this Bill believe that
to be a very valuable thing. It is designed in the
true interest not only of the author or the
publisher but of literature in general. The value
of the work in question will now have to be
considered from a literary point of view, from a
scientific point of view, an educational point of
view, or from the point of view of any other
merits. If there be passages in the book which
are objectionable or are felt to be objectionable,
it must be considered as a whole. Consideration
must be given to whether those passages are
relevant to the author's purpose, and to the
question whether he could have depicted the
life he desired to depict in any other way.

So My Lords, I present this Bill for its
three purposes; the proper amendment of the
law on obscenity; for the work it does in

protecting that which is perhaps among the most valuable thing which our country can possess, its literature, extending through very many centuries, and finally, to strengthen the law against that evil thing which ought to be most sternly suppressed, pornography."
Source: *HANSARD: House of Lords Debate Report, June 2, 1959.*

The House of Lords gave the Bill a second reading without any division, and The Obscene Publications Act received Royal Assent on 29 July 1959.

One of the changes in the law which the Bill contained, applied to orders for the forfeiture and destruction of allegedly obscene material sought by the Director of Public Prosecutions. In the Act of 1857, neither the author nor anyone concerned with the work was permitted to give evidence in court. Under the 1959 Act, they could now be heard on the ground that they were defending the article against the charge of obscenity.

The most important section of the Bill was that which stated that, in future, no one could be convicted of writing or publishing an obscene work, and no order for forfeiture should be made, if it is proved that publication of the article in question is justified as being 'for the public good on the ground that it is in the interests of science, literature, art or learning, or of other objects of general concern'. Also, the opinion of experts as to the 'literary, artistic, scientific or other merits, is admissible in evidence.

Lady Chatterley's Lover

Lawrence's novel had been the subject of three previous drafts prior to the final unexpurgated typewritten transcript submitted to Florentine publishers in March 1928. This transcript was declined publication, and Lawrence was forced to publish the first edition himself in July 1928. In August of that year, US Customs confiscated imported copies of that edition as did British authorities. It was not until 1932 that the novel was published in 'abridged' versions in the UK. In January 1960, to mark the 30th anniversary of Lawrence's death, Penguin Books agreed to publish seven additional works by DH Lawrence, (among them *Lady Chatterley's Lover)* to add to the existing thirteen titles in their catalogue.

Penguin's Chairman, Sir Alan Lane, agreed to publish the novel in full with an initial print run of 200,000 copies and a publication date of August 1960. Alerted to Penguin's intention to publish the novel, the Director of Public Prosecutions, Sir Theobald Matthew, decided to prosecute the company under the 1959 Act. This move was welcomed by Sir Reginald Manningham-Buller, the Attorney-General and Sir Jack Butler, the Solicitor-General.

The key factor in this decision to prosecute was that Penguin proposed to sell the book at the price of 3s/6d, to put it within easy reach of women and the working class. This was what the upper-middle-class male lawyers and politicians of the time refused to tolerate.

With Lawrence's use of Anglo-Saxon expletives, the explicit portrayal of sex and of course, the fact that Lady Chatterley not only commits adultery but does so with one of her husband's servants, the prosecution and the trial judge were horrified at the prospect of the working

16

class getting hold of the book.

Penguin did not expect such an aggressive response from the authorities over the publication of the novel. By the second week of August 1960, 165,000 copies of the book had been printed, of which 55,000 had been delivered to book-stores in the UK. After a meeting on the 12th August between Penguin Books and their lawyers, it was made very clear that a prosecution of the book was almost inevitable. Consequently, distribution of the book was immediately halted.

On the 15th August, Penguin's solicitor, Michael Rubinstein, wrote to a Detective Inspector Charles Monahan at Scotland Yard, London:

> *"Our Clients have instructed us to inform you that as from noon today, 12 copies of the book will be available to be handed to you at their offices. Please let us know at what time you propose to call on our Clients at their London office, when one of their directors would make himself or herself available at an hours' notice to hand the copies to you".*

Penguin's chief designer, Hans Schmoller, put together a handwritten timeline of this event in August. He noted that the books were collected by the police inspector at noon on the 16 August 1960, technically constituting 'limited publication', and the company was duly issued with a summons and charged.

The Crown, on deciding to proceed with a prosecution, realised that it would not be easy. Under the 'new' Obscene Publications Act, testimony at trial was allowed on the 'literary or other merits' of the book. Even if a jury did find the book to be obscene, that in itself would not constitute sufficient ground for conviction. It would be necessary for the prosecution to demonstrate that publication of the book was not 'in the public good'. So in order for this to be demonstrated, 'expert' testimony would have to be available to the prosecution. Consequently, the Director of Public Prosecutions, Sir Theobald Matthew, wrote to potential witnesses expressing that he would be grateful *'for your opinion as to the literary structure of the novel'*.

It is difficult to know what kind of answer he was expecting. The mere fact that he had found himself asking about such a matter suggests that the prosecution was experiencing great difficulty. The response to his request proved to be most unsuccessful with no one prepared to oblige. As a result, Matthew gave up hope of finding suitable authorities willing to testify for the prosecution.

Matthew wrote to Mervyn Griffith-Jones QC, the lead prosecution counsel.

'There is a general feeling in the literary world that this prosecution is in principle repressive and unwarranted, and in these circumstances, people whatever their views on the book may be, are not prepared to assist".

In direct contrast, Penguin's solicitor, Michael Rubinstein, approached everybody who was anybody in the world of letters and culture, totalling some 300 people. As a result, there was no shortage of eminences that were enthusiastic about the prospect of appearing in court to stand up for Lawrence, modernity, sexual liberation and good sense.

The prosecution was brought against Penguin Books Limited as the 'company' and not against the individual directors. The prosecution's case was that Lawrence's book did indeed have a tendency to deprave, in the sense of promoting impure thoughts, and was likely to mitigate against the achievement of a balanced life. Concern was raised over the social effects of its increased availability at Penguin's

affordable price. Lawrence, it was argued, had failed
to condemn the lovers' behaviour, the relationships
were immoral and the sexual part of the book, in any
case, inessential. The defence line emphasised the
estimable character and behaviour of Penguin books,
along with Lawrence's standing in the world of
literature. It stressed the value of making the novel
available to a wider public, and Penguin Books'
integrity in refusing to publish an expurgated version.

The trial of R v Penguin Books Limited took place
in Number One court at the Old Bailey in London. It lasted
for six days between 20 October and 2 November 1960.
Essentially, the trial was a 'test case' of the defence of
'public good' under Section Four of the Obscene
Publications Act 1959. The prosecution maintained that the
book '*sets upon a pedestal, promiscuous and adulterous
intercourse. It commends and indeed sets out to commend
sensuality almost as a virtue*'. The defence contended that
when viewed as a whole, the novel '*would not tend to
deprave or corrupt anyone*'. In any event, even if it were
prima facie obscene, the literary and other qualities of the
work were such that it was in the 'public good' that it
should be published.
It is to an examination of the Trial that we now turn
in Chapter Two.

CHAPTER TWO: THE TRIAL

Regina V Penguin Books Limited

Before

Mr Justice Byrne

Charged With Publishing An Obscene Article

Central Criminal Court, London

20 October – 2 November 1960

Prosecuting Counsel:	Defending Counsel:
Mr Mervyn Griffith-Jones QC	Mr Gerald Gardiner QC
Mr Alastair Morton	Mr Jeremy Hutchinson QC
	Mr Richard Du Cann

The trial opened at the Central Criminal Court in London, more famously known as the 'Old Bailey', and took place in Number One court at 10:30 am on Thursday 20 October, 1960. The first event was the calling of the jury, which in this trial consisted of nine men and three women. The trial commenced, as is the custom in English trials, with the prosecuting counsel giving an opening address to the jury outlining the case for the prosecution.

Mr Mervyn Griffith-Jones QC: Second Senior Crown Counsel

"Members of the jury, the evidence for the prosecution is this book (holding it up for display), *Lady Chatterley's Lover.* Penguin propose to publish it at the price of 3s 6d and had printed 200,000 copies of it for sale. Under the Obscene Publications Act 1959, *an article shall be deemed obscene, 'if its effect, taken as a whole, is such as to tend to deprave and corrupt persons who are likely, having regard to all its relevant circumstances, to read the matter contained in it'.* There is also another section in the Act which says that it is not an offence to publish if it is proved that the article is 'the public good', on the ground that it is in the interest of science, literature, art or learning, or other objects of general concern.

If you find the book is not obscene, that is the end of the matter, and you must acquit. But if you find that it is obscene, then you have to go on to consider is it proved that publication is in the interest of literature, science and so on. Another point you have to consider is how freely the book is going to be distributed. Is it a book published at £5 a copy, as an historical volume, or is it a book widely distributed at a price the merest infant can afford? When you have read the book, you may think that it sets upon a pedestal promiscuous and adulterous intercourse, commends sensuality almost as a virtue and encourages and advocates vulgarity of thought and language. You may think one of the ways you can test the book is to ask yourself the question, would you approve of your own son and daughter, because girls can read as well as boys, reading the book? Is it a book you would have lying in your own house? Is it a book you would wish your wife or your servant to read?

Members of the jury, you may think that the book is a picture of little else than vicious indulgence in sex and sensuality. I wish to concede that DH Lawrence is a world-recognised writer. I also concede, though not to such a great extent, that there may be some literary merit in this book, not to put it any higher. The book is about a young woman whose husband was wounded in the First World War, such that he was paralysed from the waist down and unable to have sexual intercourse. I invite you to say that in effect, the book is a description of how that woman, deprived of sex from her husband, satisfied her sexual desires, a sex-starved girl, and how she satisfied that starvation with a particularly sensual man, who happened to be her husband's gamekeeper.

There are thirteen passages of sexual intercourse in this book. The curtain is never down. One follows them not only into the bedroom, but into bed, and one remains with them there. The only variation between all thirteen occasions is the time and the place where it happens. So one starts in my lady's boudoir, one goes to a hut in the forest with a blanket laid down on the floor. We see them doing it again in the undergrowth in the forest amongst the shrubbery, and again in the undergrowth in the pouring rain, both of them stark naked and dripping with rain drops. One sees them in the keeper's cottage, first in the evening on the hearth rug, then we have to wait until dawn to see them doing it again in bed. Finally, we move the site to Bloomsbury and we have it again in a boarding house. This is the variation, the time and the place where it happens, with the emphasis always on the pleasure, the satisfaction, the sensuality.

Sex, members of the jury, is dragged in at every opportunity, even the woman's father, a Royal Academician, introduces a description of his legs and loins. The book says little about the character of any of these people, there are little more than bodies which continuously have sexual intercourse with each other. The plot, you may feel, is little more than padding, until we reach the hut again, the cottage, or the undergrowth in the forest. The word *'fuck' a*ppears thirty times, the word '*cunt*' fourteen times, the word '*balls*' thirteen times, '*shit*' six times, '*arse*' *and 'piss'* three times each. Penguin Books have stated it had taken twenty years for it to be possible to publish the 'unmutilated' version of *Lady Chatterley's Lover.* You, members of the jury will have to say whether it has taken thirty or whether it will take still longer".

During the trial, the prosecution called their one and only witness, Detective Inspector Charles Monahan. He stated that he had been given a dozen copies of the book in Penguin's offices. This fact established evidence of 'limited publication' on the part of Penguin Books."

Defence Opening Address to the Jury: Mr Gerald Gardiner QC

"Members of the jury, you have been told that this book is full of descriptions of sexual intercourse and so it is. That it is full of four-letter words, and so it is. You may ask yourself at once how comes it that reputable publishers apparently after considerable thought and quite deliberately, are publishing an appalling book of the nature which has been described to us? Penguin Books began in 1935 under a man called Lane, a man who thought that people like himself, who were not very rich, should be able to buy books. They started with a novel and some detective stories, then came classics, and translations of masterpieces of literature, all costing sixpence. Twenty-five years later, they had sold 250 million books. They have published the whole of Shakespeare, most of Shaw, they had published fourteen books by DH Lawrence and now they intended to publish the rest, including *Lady Chatterley's Lover.*

This book has had unfortunately, a history. It was written in 1928 but it had not been possible to publish it at that time. There are many books circulating in London now which nobody would have thought ought to have been printed even twenty years ago. There have been expurgated editions of *Lady Chatterley,,* and there would have been nothing to stop Penguin years ago publishing one, but they had always refused to publish a 'mutilated' book. The expurgated edition was not the book Lawrence wrote. One could have expurgated editions of Hamlet and the Canterbury Tales, but they would not be the books Shakespeare or Chaucer wrote.

Dictionary definitions of 'to deprave and to corrupt' are expressed as; to make morally bad; to pervert; to deteriorate; to make rotten; to infect; to render unsound; to debase; to defile; So, for a book to be obscene within the meaning of the law, it must obviously effect a change of character, a leading-on of the reader, to do something wrong, which he would not otherwise have done.

When you have read the book, you will see certain things which the author was aiming at. Mr Griffith-Jones has suggested that this was a book which contained thirteen descriptions of physical intercourse, and that the only variation between them was the time and the place. I would suggest that you will find exactly the opposite. Here is a book about England of the Twenties.

Lawrence's message is that the society of his day was sick, the result of the machine age, and the importance which everybody attached to money, and to the extent to which mind has been stressed at the expense of the body, and that what we ought to do was to re-establish the personal relationships. As one of the greatest things, the author thought was the relationship of a man and woman in love, and their physical union formed as essential part of a relation which was normal and wholesome, and not something to be ashamed of, but something to be discussed openly and frankly. If a man is going to write a book of that kind, and deal with the physical relation between the sexes, it is necessary to describe what he means. I submit that the descriptions of physical union were necessary for what Lawrence was trying to say.

It is quite true that the book includes what are called four-letter words, and it is quite plain that what the author intended was to drag these words out of the rather shameful connotation which they had achieved since Victorian times. The attitude of shame with which large numbers of people have always viewed sex in any form has reduced us to the position where it is not at all easy for fathers and mothers to find words to describe to their children the physical union. The author thought that if he used what had been part of our spoken speech for about six hundred years, he could purify it. Whether he succeeded or not in his attempt to purify these words by dragging them into the light of day, there is nothing in the words themselves which can 'deprave or corrupt'. If these words can deprave or corrupt, then ninety-five per cent of the Army, Navy and Air Force are past redemption! While parts of the book may (and I do not doubt will) shock you, there is nothing in the book which will in fact do anybody any harm. No one would suggest that the Director of Public Prosecutions would become depraved by reading the book, that counsel, nor witnesses, no one would suggest that the judge and jury would become corrupt, it is always someone else, it is never ourselves."

The opening speeches having been delivered, the

judge directed that the jury should attend court to read the book within the confines of the Jury Room. Consequently, the trial was adjourned for one week to facilitate the jury's reading of the book.

The trial resumed on Thursday 27 October as Day Two of the trial, and lasted for a further five days finishing on Wednesday 2 November 1960.

The first three days were occupied with statements given by 35 defence witnesses. These included, eight university academics, fourteen authors, journalists and editors, three publishers, four Anglican churchmen and two school teachers. Other testimonies came from a lawyer, a Labour politician, an educational psychologist and finally, a Cambridge English graduate.

Witnesses Appearing For The Defence

University Academics
Graham Hough, Lecturer in English, Christ's College, Cambridge.
Helen Gardner, Reader in Renaissance English Literature, Oxford.
Joan Bennett, Lecturer in English, Girton College, Cambridge.
Vivian de Sola Pinto, Professor of English, Nottingham University.
Richard Hoggart, Lecturer in English, Leicester University.
Raymond Williams, Tutor in English, Oxford University.
Kenneth Muir, Professor of English, Liverpool University.
Noel Annan, Provost, King's College, Cambridge.

Authors, Journalists and Editors
Dame Rebecca West	C Day-Lewis
Veronica Wedgwood	Stephen Potter
Edward Williams	Janet Smith
Edward M Forster	John Connell

Walter Allen	Kenneth Young
Anne Scott-James	Alastair Hetherington
Jack Lambert	Dilys Powell

Publishers
William Emrys Williams, Penguin's Editor-in-Chief.
Sir Allen Lane, Founder of Penguin.

Bookseller
Stanley Unwin

Anglican Churchmen
John Robinson, Bishop of Woolwich.
Stephen Hopkinson, Vicar of St Katherine Cree, London.
Richard Milford, Editor: London Churchman.
Donald Tytler, Director of Religious Education, Diocese of Birmingham.

School Teachers
Francis Cammaerts, Alleyne's Grammar School, Stevenage.
Sarah Beryl Jones, Classics Mistress, Keighley Girls Grammar School.

Norman St John Stevas, Academic Barrister and future MP.
Roy Jenkins, Labour MP.
James Hemming, Educational Psychologist.
Bernadine Wall, Cambridge English Graduate.

When the trial re-commenced on Thursday 27 October, the first three witnesses for the defence - Hough, Gardner and Bennett - were all English scholars who each confirmed Lawrence's standing as a novelist. They refuted the prosecution's suggestion that the work was no more than a story of sexual encounters between Constance Chatterley and the gamekeeper Mellors. They also justified Lawrence's use of 'four-letter-words' as integral to the novel's overall literary effect.

DAY TWO: Thursday 27 October 1960

Witness: Mr Graham Hough, Lecturer in English and Fellow of Christ's College, Cambridge. DH Lawrence specialist.

Mr Gardiner: When did you first read the unexpurgated edition of *Lady Chatterley's Lover?*
Mr Hough: In about 1940.
Mr Gardiner: Will you tell us something about Lawrence's place in English literature?
Mr Hough: He is generally recognised as being one of the most important novelists of this century. I should put him with Hardy and with Conrad and George Eliot.
Mr Gardiner: How many books have been written about DH Lawrence?
Mr Hough: About eight hundred published.
Mr Gardiner: How do you rank Lady Chatterley's Lover?
Mr Hough: I don't think it's the best of Lawrence's novels, but not the least good either. About fifth place, he wrote nine.
Mr Gardiner: Will you tell us what is the theme or meaning of this book?
Mr Hough: It is an attempt to give a sympathetic understanding to a very painful, intricate human situation. The book is in fact concerned with the relationships between men and women, with their sexual relations and with the nature of marriage, these are matters of great importance to us all.
Mr Gardiner: It has been claimed that sex is dragged in at every opportunity and the plot is little more than padding.
Mr Hough: I totally disagree. If true, this would be an attack on the integrity and honesty of the author, but it is quite false. In the first place, it is a matter of simple

numerical proportion, the sexual passages occupy no more than about thirty pages of the whole book, a book of some three hundred pages. No man in his senses is going to write a book of three hundred pages as 'mere padding', and then the literary merit of the non-sexual passages is very high.

Mr Gardiner: It has been suggested that the book puts upon a pedestal promiscuous and adulterous intercourse.

Mr Hough: Promiscuity hardly comes into it. It is very much condemned by Lawrence. It is true that at the centre of the book there is an adulterous situation, that is true of a great deal of the literature of Europe.

Mr Gardiner: It has been said that the only variation in the scenes of intercourse is in the places they occur. Do you agree?

Mr Hough: No I don't. They show the development of Connie Chatterley's awareness of her nature. They are not repetitive, they are different and necessary to the author's purpose.

Mr Gardiner: How far are the descriptions of intercourse relevant or necessary?

Mr Hough: They are extremely necessary. Lawrence was trying to show sexual relationships more clearly than is usually done in fiction. Lawrence was making a bold experiment.

Mr Gardiner: How far are the four-letter words relevant or necessary?

Mr Hough: May I answer that by explaining why they are in? In Lawrence's view, there is no proper language to talk about sexual matters. They are either discussed in clinical terms, which deprive them of all emotional content, or they are described in words that are usually thought to be coarse or obscene. Lawrence wanted to find a language in which sex could be discussed plainly and not irreverently, and to do so he tried to redeem the normally obscene words by using them in a context that is entirely serious. I don't myself think that this is successful, but that is what he was trying to do. In treating sex in this way, Lawrence had few precedents before him. He had to try to find a way through.

Mr Gardiner: Do you spend a great deal of time teaching young people?

Mr Hough: I do.

Mr Gardiner: And you have a daughter of eighteen and a son of twelve?

Mr Hough: I have.

Cross-Examination Mr Griffith- Jones

Mr Griffith-Jones: Do you know a lady called Esther Forbes?

Mr Hough: No, I'm afraid not.

Mr Griffith-Jones: Are you familiar with a magazine called '*Encounter*'?

Mr Hough: *Encounter?* Yes, I am.

Mr Griffith-Jones: Is *Encounter* a serious publication?

Mr Hough: Reasonably so.

Mr Griffith-Jones: Would you agree with this American lady writing in *Encounter* that this novel is 'a dreary, sad performance, with some passages of hilarious low comedy', and written with much inflamed apostolic solemnity?

Mr Hough: I think that this is an eccentric opinion.

Mr Griffith-Jones: Because you do not agree with it? Do you agree with this view of Lady Chatterley: 'She is merely a moral imbecile, she is stupid'?

Mr Hough: Connie is not stupid, she is an emancipated young woman of the period, friendly, warm-hearted, patient.

Mr Griffith-Jones: What do you mean, warm-hearted, filled with sex?

Mr Hough: No, this is not what I mean.

Mr Griffith-Jones: Miss Katherine Porter, the American writer says the book is 'a blood chilling anatomy of the activities of the rutting season between two rather dull persons'. Do you think that is a view one is entitled to hold?

Mr Hough: Oh, anyone is entitled to hold any view. This one disposes of the argument that the book excites the sexual passions.

Mr Griffith-Jones: Is this book the feeble daydream of a dying man sitting under the umbrella pines indulging his sexual fantasies?

Mr Hough: Lawrence died two years after publication.

Mr Griffith-Jones: (First read aloud a passage on page 204 of the Penguin edition) We have had two four-letter words appearing repeatedly in twelve lines, is that a realistic conversation between a gamekeeper and a baronet's wife?

Mr Hough: I don't think so. I think as a passage this is a failure.

Mr Griffith-Jones: You grant me this much? In this book which is of such merit, there is at least one passage which is a failure.

Mr Hough: There are several.

Mr Griffith-Jones: The entire rest of the book, let's face it, is about sex? Even the old nurse, Mrs Bolton, is dragged in without any point at all, so that Sir Clifford may feel her breasts?

Mr Hough: There is very much point. This is the most relevant. The decay of Clifford is shown to have become like an unpleasant child.

Mr Griffith-Jones: Is there any particular literary or sociological advantage in having this described?

Mr Hough: Yes, I think there is. These are representations of false and wrong sexual attitudes, and this is an important part of the book.

Mr Griffith-Jones: Where do the good attitudes come in?

Mr Hough: Well, in the relationship between Connie and Mellors, who really loved one another.

Mr Griffith-Jones: Are you an expert on good sexual relationships?

Mr Hough: I do not not share the sexual ethics of DH Lawrence. I was never a disciple of his doctrine, but I think it is important and should be clearly stated.

Witness: Miss Helen Gardner, Reader in Renaissance English Literature, St Hilda's College, Oxford.

Mr Gardiner: It has been said, that the four-letter words form the whole subject matter of the prosecution, and that one word occurred thirty times?

Miss Gardner: I do not think words are brutal or disgusting in themselves, they are brutal if used in such a sense or context. The very fact that this word is used so frequently in this book means that with every use, the overall shock is diminished. By the time one has read the last page, one feels that Lawrence has gone far to redeem this word.

Mr Gardiner: What do you gather was Lawrence's original intention?

Miss Gardner: To make us feel that the sexual act is not shameful and the word used in its original sense is not shameful either. Those passages succeed in doing something extraordinary with such courage and vision to put into verbal media experiences that are difficult to verbalise.

Mr Gardiner: Do you feel any embarrassment in discussing this book in a mixed class?

Miss Gardner: Good gracious, no.

Mr Gardiner: What, in your view, is the theme?

Miss Gardner: I think Lawrence felt very deeply the degrading conditions in which many people lived without beauty or joy. He thought the most fundamental wrong was in the relationship between men and women, in sex, he thought through a better relationship the whole of society might be revivified. It is a remarkable though not wholly successful novel, and though it doesn't rank with the greatest of Lawrence's work, I think certain passages are amongst his greatest.

The prosecution did not cross-examine this witness.

Witness: Mrs Joan Bennett - Lecturer in English and Fellow of Girton College, Cambridge

Mr Gardiner: What was Lawrence's view of life?

Mrs Bennett: Lawrence's view was that the physical life was of great importance. Many people lived poor emasculated lives, they only lived with one half of themselves, Lawrence dealt with sex seriously, very seriously. Promiscuous intercourse was shown as unsatisfactory, giving no fulfilment or joy, as being rather disgusting. He thought that marriage was a complete relationship not quite in the legal sense, but a union between two people for a lifetime was of the highest importance, of almost sacred importance.

Mr Gardiner: And have you got one son, three daughters and eight grand-children?

Mrs Bennett: I have.

Cross-Examination: Mr Griffith-Jones

Mr Griffith-Jones: Does not this book show a picture of a woman who has sexual relationships with people who are not her husband?

Mrs Bennett: Yes.

Mr Griffith-Jones: Does this adulterous intercourse show a regard for marriage as it is generally understood by the 'average reader'?

Mrs Bennett: What average reader? If you mean an intelligent child?

Mr Griffith-Jones: If you can come down to our humbler

level from your academic heights, will you answer my question. Does this book show regard for marriage?

Mrs Bennett: In what sense do you mean marriage?

The judge Intervened here: Lawful wedlock, madam.

Mrs Bennett: Lawrence believed it can be, as I think the law allows, broken in certain conditions?

Mr Griffith-Jones: Is not that precisely what Lawrence himself did? He ran off with somebody else's wife, did he not?

Re-Examination

Mr Gardiner: Did DH Lawrence's one and only marriage last his lifetime?

Mrs Bennett: It did.

Witness. Dame Rebecca West - Author and Literary Critic

Outlining the basis of the book, she stated that the story of Lady Chatterley was designed as an allegory; the baronet and his impotence were a symbol of the impotent culture of our time which had become sterile and unhelpful to man's deepest needs. The love affair with the gamekeeper was a return of the soul to a more intense life. Lawrence was not a fanciful writer; he knew he was writing about something quite real - he saw that in every country in the world, there were populations who had lost touch with life and who could be exploited. One could find individual passages which appear to have no literary merit. Lawrence was a man without a background of formal education, and he had one great defect which impairs this book - he had no sense of humour. A lot of scenes are ludicrous. But despite the ugly things and the ugly words, it is still a good book.

No Cross-Examination by the Prosecution

Witness. Dr John Robinson, Anglican Bishop of Woolwich

Mr Griffith-Jones: I submit that the Bishop cannot be heard, his qualifications do not entitle him to give evidence about the book's literary merits.

Mr Gardiner: The Bishop has come to give evidence on its 'ethical merits'.

Mr Griffith-Jones: Ethical merits are not mentioned in the Obscene Publications Act.

Mr Gardiner: (Addressing the judge) My Lord, the Act mentions art or learning or other objects of general concern.

The judge: I agree with you, ethics must be considered an object of general concern.

Bishop Robinson: Lawrence did not have a Christian valuation of sex, and the kind of relationships depicted in the book are not necessarily of the kind I should regard as ideal. But what Lawrence is trying to do, I think, is to portray the sex relationship as something 'sacred'. I think Lawrence tried to portray this relationship in the real sense as an act of 'holy communion', in a lower case. For him, flesh was 'sacramental'. Lawrence's descriptions of sexual relationships cannot be taken out of the context of his whole quite astonishing sensitivity to the beauty and value of all 'organic relationships'. Some of the descriptions of nature in the book seem to me extraordinary beautiful, and to portray an attitude to the whole organic world in which he saw sex as the culmination.

Mr Gardiner: Can you make a distinction between the book as it is, and as it would be with the sexual passages left out?

Bishop Robinson: I think the effect of that would be to suggest that what Lawrence was doing was something sordid and could be put before the public only if the passages about sex were eliminated. I think this is a false view. I think neither in intention nor in effect, is the book depraving. It has been said it puts promiscuous and adulterous intercourse on a pedestal. That seems a distorted view. In the last pages there is a tremendous and most moving advocacy of chastity. How can men want wearisomely to philander?

Cross-Examination: Mr Griffith-Jones

Mr Griffith-Jones: Do you tell us that this book is a valuable work on ethics?

Bishop Robinson: It is not a treatise on marriage, but Lawrence made it clear that he was not against marriage relationships.

Mr Griffith-Jones: I don't want to be offensive to you, but you are not here to make speeches. Just answer my question. Are you asking the jury to accept this book as a valuable work on ethics?

Bishop Robinson: I would not say it had an 'instructive' value.

Mr Griffith-Jones: Is it a book Christians ought to read?

The judge: (Intervening) Does it portray the love of an immoral woman?

Bishop Robinson: It portrays the love of a woman in an immoral relationship, so far as adultery is an immoral relationship.

Mr Griffith-Jones: Is it a book Christians ought to read?

Bishop Robinson: Yes, I think it is.

Witness: Sir William Emrys Williams - Editor-in-Chief Penguin Books

Mr Griffith-Jones: Will you explain why you printed 200,000 copies of this book?

Sir William: That is nothing out of the ordinary. An average first printing of a Penguin would be 40,000 to 50,000 copies, but for some books we print as many as 250,000.

Mr Griffith-Jones: Why did you not think of putting in rows of asterisks?

Sir William: That would make it a dirty book.

Mr Griffith-Jones: What about dashes for the four-letter words?

Sir William: That would make for unwholesomeness.

Mr Griffith-Jones: Do you think you could have sold a large number of copies of an expurgated edition?

Sir William: Quite the same number.

Witness: Mr Norman St John-Stevas - Academic Barrister and Legal Adviser

Mr Hutchinson (Defence Counsel): How would you describe Lawrence as a writer?

Mr St John-Stevas: Lawrence was essentially concerned to purge, cleanse and reform. I have been horrified by the representation of him in some newspapers which I think he wouldn't have deigned to read. I have had the misfortune to have to read through a vast number of books of a pornographic and obscene nature, and I find it difficult to make comparisons with *Lady Chatterley,* so great is the gulf between them.

Mr Hutchinson: Do you find the book consistent with the tenets of your own Catholic faith?

Mr St John-Stevas: Quite consistent. Of course Lawrence was neither a Christian nor a Catholic. One could say he was a writer essentially in the Catholic tradition. I mean by that tradition that the sex instinct is good in itself, is implanted in man by God, is one of his greatest gifts. This tradition was opposed by the movement which started at the Reformation and has grown in Protestant minds, that sex is something which is wrong, which is essentially evil.

Witness: Miss Sarah Beryl Jones – Classic Mistress and Senior Librarian, Keighley Girls Grammar School

Mr Gardiner: Do girls grow up earlier now than they used to?

Miss Jones: In my experience, yes.

Mr Gardiner: Is there a good deal of literature available to them on sexual matters?

Miss Jones: There are technical works, and there are what you might call dirty books.

Mr Gardiner: How far do girls understand the four-letter words?

Miss Jones: I have inquired of a number of a number of girls after they left school, and most of them had been acquainted with them since the age of ten.

Mr Gardiner: Has *Lady Chatterley's Lover* any educational value?

Miss Jones: Considerable value if taken at the right age which is normally after seventeen, because it deals honestly and openly with problems of sex which are very real to the girls themselves. Girls are very good at knowing what is good for them. Girls read what they want to read, and they don't read what they don't want to read...

Witness: Dr Clifford James Hemming – Educational Psychologist

Dr Hemming: Young people reading *Lady Chatterley* might find themselves for the first time, confronted with a concept of sex which includes compassion and tenderness. Young people nowadays are subject to constant insinuation of shallow and corrupting values. Books and papers tell the young girl that if she has the right proportions, wears the right clothes, uses the right cosmetics, she will become irresistible to men, and that this is the supreme achievement of woman, to become irresistible to men. And as far as the men are concerned, it is suggested that to have a pretty woman in your arms is the supreme thrill of life, and to seduce a woman is manful in yourself and something to envy in others. The contents of *Lady Chatterley* are an antidote. They show all that makes sex human.

Mr Gardiner: Are the detailed descriptions justified? Are they of any sociological value?

Dr Hemming: Oh yes, it is now recognised that for young people to grow up and marry with brutish and ashamed attitudes is most harmful. The rejection of our bodies can lead to mental ill health. This book would act as a positive antidote to those promiscuous and dehumanising influences.

Cross-Examination: Mr Griffith-Jones

Mr Griffith-Jones: Let us see what amounts to an antidote. (He reads a passage from the novel.) Is that an antidote to promiscuous sex among young people?
Dr Hemming: Yes, that was a description of what was happening just before the act of intercourse.
Mr Griffith-Jones: Yes, that was promiscuous intercourse by Lady Chatterley?

Dr. Hemming: Yes, but it is quite different from the street-corner promiscuity which is one of our problems today.

Mr Griffith-Jones: I was not limiting my meaning to street corners. Is there anything to suggest that she wouldn't have gone on and on, from man to man, until she found someone who satisfied her?

Dr Hemming: That is a conjectural question. I do not believe she would have led that kind of life.

Mr Griffith-Jones: Here we have another one of the bouts, (he reads another passage out). Does that strengthen the antidote much? Does it?

Dr Hemming: I don't see why not.

Mr Griffith-Jones: As he found her. What do you think these words mean?

Dr Hemming: Getting into closer intimacy.

Mr Griffith-Jones: What do you mean?

Dr Hemming: What Lawrence means.

Mr Griffith-Jones: What do you mean by that?

Dr Hemming: A continuation of the physical act of love.

Mr Griffith-Jones: What do you mean by that? I shall go on asking you until you tell us in plain English words what you think that means?

Dr Hemming: He was caressing her.

Mr Griffith-Jones: Where?

Dr Hemming: It doesn't say.

Witness - Mr Richard Hoggart: Senior Lecturer in English, Leicester University

Examination by Mr Jeremy Hutchinson: Junior Defence Counsel

Mr Hoggart had referred to *Lady Chatterley* as a highly virtuous if not a 'puritanical' book. Mr Hutchinson invites him to enlarge on that view.

Mr Hoggart: I was thinking of the whole movement of the book, of Lawrence's enormous insistence on arriving at relationships of integrity. I was struck on re-reading it to realise how much of it is contemporary; it tells us a great deal about our society at a level which we do not usually probe, and with an insight which we do not usually see. It makes you consider your relationship to society, it teaches you to question your place and your being.

Mr Hutchinson: It has been suggested that the only variations in the sexual descriptions lay in where they took place.

Mr Hoggart: A gross misreading. I don't mean highbrow reading. I mean an honest reading.

Mr Hutchinson asked him about repetition of words.

Mr Hoggart: Indeed, yes. It's one of Lawrence's characteristics, and one he uses to great effect. He hammered home and almost recreated words. Shakespeare repeated 'nothing' five times in one passage.

Mr Hutchinson: Are the four-letter words genuine and necessary?

Mr Hoggart: They are totally characteristic of many people, and I would like to say not only working-class people, because that would be wrong. They are used very freely indeed, far more freely than many of us know. Fifty yards from this court this morning, I heard a man say that word three times as I passed him, one, two, three. I heard him. He must have been very angry. These are common words; if you work on a building site, as I have done, you will hear them frequently. But the man I heard this morning and the men on the building site use this word as a word of contempt, and one of the most horrifying things to Lawrence was that the word used for sex has become a term of violent abuse, and has totally lost its meaning. He wanted to re-establish the proper meaning of it. When I first read it, the first effect was one of some shock, obviously because it is not used in polite literature. But as one read,

41

one found the word losing that shock. We have no word in English which is not either an abstraction or has become an evasive euphemism for this act; we are constantly running away from it or dissolving into dots. I realised that it is we who are wrong. Lawrence was wanting to show what one does in the most simple, neutral way. Just like that, with no snigger or dirt. That is what one does.

Cross-Examination by Mr Griffith-Jones

Mr Griffith-Jones: You described this as a 'puritanical' book. Is that your genuine and considered view?
Mr Hoggart: Yes.
Mr Griffith-Jones: I think I must have lived my life under a misapprehension of the word 'puritanical'. Will you help me?
Mr Hoggart: Yes I will. Many people do live their lives under a misapprehension of the meaning of 'puritanical'. In Britain, and for a long time, the word has pretended to mean somebody who is against anything which is pleasurable, particularly sex, but the proper meaning of it to an historian is somebody who belongs to the tradition of British puritanism and the main weight of that is an intense sense of responsibility for one's conscience. In that sense, the book is puritanical.
Mr Griffith-Jones: I am obliged to you for the lecture. (He then reads a sexual passage from the book.) Is that puritanical?
Mr Hoggart: Yes, heavily with conscience.
Mr Griffith-Jones: I am not asking you if it is heavy with conscience. I am asking you if it is puritanical?
Mr Hoggart: Yes. It is one of the side issues of puritanism.
Mr Griffith-Jones: I should have thought that could be answered without a lecture. This is the Old Bailey, and not Leicester University. (He then read an extraordinary page

about the source of life.) The weight of a man's balls -
puritanical?
Mr Hoggart: Yes, it is puritanical in its reverence.
Mr Griffith-Jones: Reverence for what? The Balls?
Mr Hoggart: Indeed, yes.

Hoggart's arguments were reiterated by subsequent
witnesses, including EM Forster, the famous writer, and
Roy Jenkins the politician and architect of the 1959 Act.
Penguin's founder, Allen Lane, took the stand. In reply to
Jeremy Hutchinson, defence counsel, he explained the aims
of his company (a University Press in paperbacks), and his
reasons for publishing an unexpurgated edition of *Lady
Chatterley.* He highlighted its importance for a complete set
of Lawrence's work, the company policy of not producing
edited editions, and the opportunity presented by the
legislation of 1959.

Penguin's contribution to British cultural life was
subsequently endorsed by Lane's fellow publisher Stanley
Unwin, who was followed by Dilys Powell, who argued for
the superiority of Lawrence's depictions of sex when
compared with many of those in contemporary cinema.
Cecil Day-Lewis defended Connie Chatterley against the
prosecution's charge of immorality.

The potentially damaging effects of her and
Mellor's conduct on the young was in turn, dismissed by
the educationalist Donald Tytler, who claimed that the
novel was an important corrective to an increasingly
common view that sex was 'unimportant' and hence
promiscuity 'the normal course'.

The final word went to one young reader, Bernadine
Wall, who began by describing the obvious shortcomings of
the novel in its censored form. Asked what she made of
Lawrence's language in the unexpurgated version, she
replied that his choice of words contained no surprises as 'I
knew all of them at that time'.

Tuesday 1st November, 1960. Day Five

Defence Closing Address to the Jury: Mr Gerald Gardiner QC

"Members of the jury, it might be suggested that you should ignore the evidence given by professors of literature, by people who are living rarefied lives and are not really in touch with ordinary people. Indeed, no higher class of experts could have been called on any similar occasion. The most important single fact here was that Parliament had expressively provided that evidence may be called both by the defence and by the prosecution. Yet, when the prosecution's turn came to call evidence, they called none at all. Not one single witness has been found to say anything against Lawrence or his book. We have only got to go by what Mr Griffith-Jones said himself when opening the case. Hardly any question has been put to witnesses by the prosecution about the book as a whole. The technique has been that used before the new Act, to read out a particular passage, and then say, is that moral?

This is a book about human beings, about real people, and I protest at the statements that have been made about the characters, about Constance as though she was a sort of nymphomaniac. When it is said that this is just a book about adultery, one wonders how there can be things which people cannot see? I suppose somewhere there may be a mind which would describe Antony and Cleopatra as a play about adultery, the story of a sex-starved Roman soldier, copulating with an Egyptian queen.

As a book published at 3s 6d, *Lady Chatterley* will be available to the general public, and it may well be said that everyone will rush to buy it. This is always the effect of a wrong prosecution. Witnesses have been asked if it was a book they would like their wife or servant to read. This may have been consciously or unconsciously, an echo of the Bench of years ago: "...it would never do to let the members of the working class to read this". I don't want to upset the prosecution by suggesting there are a certain number of people who do not have servants!

This whole attitude is one Penguin Books was formed to fight against. It is the attitude that it is alright to publish a special edition at five or ten guineas, but quite wrong to let people who are less well-off read what those other people read. Is not everyone whether their income is ten pounds or twenty pounds a week, equally interested in the society in which we live and in the problems of our relationships, including sexual relationships?

It would be very easy to say to you for counsel for the prosecution, "You and I are ordinary chaps, don't bother about those experts, they don't really know what goes on in the world at all". Lawrence, members of the jury, was a man of the people. There are students of literature in all walks of life. If it is right that the book should be read, it should be available to the man working in a factory, as it is to the teacher working in a school. In England, we have before banned books by Hardy, GB Shaw, Wilde, Joyce and even Epstein's statues.

But is Lawrence to be always confined to dirty bookshops? This would be the greatest irony in literary history. A book is not obscene merely because part of its subject matter is a relationship between people who are not married, or who are married to someone else. If that were so, ninety per cent of English literature is obscene.

Can it be seriously suggested that anyone's character will be changed by reading words that they already know? I submit that the defence has shown on the 'balance of probabilities', that it is for the public good that this book should be generally available. If this is not a book to which the section of the new Act applies, then it is difficult to conceive of any book by such an author to which it can apply. We are a country known throughout the world for our literature and our democratic institutions. It is strange indeed that this is the only country where this Englishman's work cannot be read.

Lawrence lived and died suffering from the public opinion caused by the banning of this book, that he had written a piece of pure pornography. For the first time this case has enabled the book to be dragged out into the light of day. The slur was never justified. All the time the book was a passionate and sincere work of a moralist who believed he had a message for us in the society in which we live. Whether we agree with what he had in view or not, is it not time we rescued Lawrence's name from the quite unjust reputation and allowed our people, his people, to judge for themselves? I leave Lawrence's reputation and the reputation of Penguin Books with confidence in your hands."

Prosecution Closing Address to the Jury – Mr Mervyn Griffith-Jones QC

"Members of the jury, this is a case of immense importance and its effects will go far beyond the actual question which you have to decide. It has been emphasised that you have heard no witnesses called by the prosecution. It may sound a good point to reiterate again and again, but it is an empty point, and not the kind of argument on which you are to decide the case. The law restricts me to calling evidence only as to the 'literary, artistic and other merits' of the book.

As to the merit of the book as literature, I have from the first conceded that Lawrence was a great writer. These are matters upon which the prosecution never sought to argue, and upon which it would have been wholly irrelevant and redundant for me to call evidence.

On whether the book is of educational or sociological merit, I am happy to leave that aspect to the book itself. I cannot believe that you, or any other jury, would wish evidence to be called simply to hear these words. This book is not a great educational document, nor is it of great sociological value.

Members of the jury, there are standards are there not? These must be standards which we are to maintain: standards of morality, language and conduct, which are essential to the well-being of our society. They must be instilled in all of us, and at the earliest possible age, standards of respect for the conventions, for the kind of conduct society approves, for other people's feelings, and there must be instilled in all of us standards of restraint. You have only to read your papers and see day by day, the results of unbridled sex. It is all for lack of standards, lack of restraint, lack of mental and moral discipline.

It is true as Mr Gardiner has anticipated, that I would urge upon you that you alone will have to decide, and not the various witnesses whose views you have heard. You will not be brow-beaten by these witnesses, you will judge the case as ordinary men and women with your feet firmly planted on the ground. Were the views you have heard from these most eminent and academic ladies and gentlemen really so much value as to views which you, without perhaps the eminence and the academic learning, possess yourselves? I do not question the integrity and sincerity of those witnesses, but suggest that they all have got a 'bee in their bonnet' about this book. When one sees some of them launching themselves at the first opportunity, according to their vocation, one cannot help feeling that, sincerely and honestly as they feel, they feel in such a way that common sense perhaps has gone by the board.

One witness said that sex was treated 'on a holy basis'. Can this be a realistic view? Is that a way a boy leaving school would read it? The Bishop of Woolwich went one better, and called it something as sacred as an act of 'Holy Communion'. Do you think that is the way girls working in a factory will read the book in their luncheon

47

break? Or does it put the Bishop wholly out of touch with the large percentage of people who will buy the book at 3s/6d?

Will you look at page 258. It is a passage which I have not, and I do not think anybody has referred to during the course of cross-examination, or indeed at any time during this trial. It describes what is called the 'night of sensual pleasure'. It is not very easy to know what in fact, he is driving at in the passage. I suggest that Miss Rebecca West is capable of reading what she said into the book, but is that typical of the effect that book will have on the average reader? Are they going to see an allegory in it? Is the baronet and his impotence going to be read by them as a symbol? One wonders whether one is talking in the same language?

Members of the jury, is there any moral teaching in the book at all? How can there be when right until the end, when they decide to get their respective divorces, not a single word is spoken between them during the thirteen bouts other than sex. All they have done before they decide to run away with each other, is to copulate thirteen times. It has been suggested that the shock of using the foul words wore off as one got used to it. Is that not a terrible thing if we forget the shock of using this language? It is for the jury to decide this case, and not for the so-called experts.

This book has to be read not as bishops and lecturers read it, but as ordinary men and women read it, people without any lectern or academic qualifications. Do you think, as I submit, that its effect on the average person must be to 'deprave', to lead them into false conceptions, to lower their general standard of thought, conduct and decency, and must be the opposite to encourage that restraint in sexual matters which is so all-important in present times? And if you decide that it has a tendency to deprave, then you have to ask yourselves what 'public good' is being done by this book to outweigh the harm. Is there such a public need in the interest of public good for the publication of this document? There can be but one answer."

Judge's Summing-Up to the Jury – Mr Justice Byrne

"In these days the world seems to be full of experts. There is no subject you can think of where there is not to be found an expert who will be able to deal, or says he will be able to deal, with the situation. But the criminal law is based on a view that a jury is responsible for the facts and not the experts. There is no intent to deprave necessary to be proved in order that this offence should be committed. The intention is quite irrelevant. This book is put on the market at 3s 6d a copy, which is by no means an excessive price in these days when there are not only high wages but high pocket money. Once a book gets into circulation, it does not spend its time in the rarefied atmosphere of some academic institutions, it finds its way into the book shops and onto stalls, and into public libraries where it is available to all and sundry to read. The book has been said to be a moral tract, a virtuous and puritanical production, and a book that Christians ought to read. What do you think about that?

Is it right to say that the story is one of a woman who first of all before she was married, had sexual intercourse, and then after marriage, when her husband had met with disaster in the war, and became confined to a wheelchair? She was living with her husband in this dreary place called Wragley, and committed adultery on two occasions with somebody called Michallis, while her husband was downstairs in the same house. After that she proceeded to have adulterous intercourse with her husband's gamekeeper. And that is described you may think, in the most lurid way, and the whole sensuality and passion of the various occasions is fully and completely described. You will have to consider the tendency that this

49

book will have on the moral outlook of people who buy it, people possibly without any knowledge of Lawrence, or of literature, and people perhaps quite young, the youth of the country.

If you are satisfied that the book is obscene, you must go on the further question; are the merits of the book, as a novel, so high that they outbalance the obscenity so its publication is for the 'public good'? I would repeat the observation made by Mr Griffith-Jones who said 'Keep your feet on the ground'. In other words, do not allow yourselves to get lost in the higher realms of literature, education, sociology and ethics.

One witness, Mrs Bennett said "A reader who is capable of understanding Lawrence could get much of what his view is". Who, members of the jury, are the people capable of understanding Lawrence?

You have to think of people with no literary background, with little or no learning. It has been said that the book does not deal simply and solely with sexual relationships, but that it deals with other matters, such as the hard lives people are living. Whether you find there is very much in the book about that or not is for you to say. You may ask yourselves whether, unless a person is an authority on literature, he would be able to read into the book, the many different things the many witnesses say he intended to be in the book. Mrs Bennett said that Lawrence believed that marriage, not in the legal sense, but the union of two people for a lifetime was of the highest importance.

Members of the jury, what is marriage if it is not in the legal sense? What are they talking about? This is a Christian country, and right through Christianity, there has been lawful marriage, even if it is only before a registrar.

The Bishop of Woolwich said Lawrence was trying to portray the sex relationship as something 'sacramental'. Do you find that the author was trying to portray sex as something sacramental? Do you find that the relationship between Lady Chatterley and the gamekeeper was really moral, or were they really having sexual intercourse and enjoying it?

You heard one witness say that it is possible to feel 'reverence for a man's balls'. What do you make of that? Does it coincide with your view of the matter? Well members of the jury, there it is. You must ask yourselves whether, as you read the book, you find you can agree with all the things the witnesses said that Lawrence was trying to say. You are not bound by the evidence. You have to make up your own minds".

On the afternoon of Wednesday 2 November 1960, after three hours of deliberation, the jury returned a verdict of Not Guilty, ending one of the most famous socially significant criminal trials of the twentieth century. Gerald Gardiner, counsel for the defence, claimed that the prosecution's argument had been overwhelmed by the calibre and consistency of the defence witnesses. He also drew the jury's attention to the fact that they were not judging a pornographic bookseller, but a highly regarded publisher whose directors clearly did not consider the novel to be obscene.

Mervyn Griffith-Jones for the prosecution stated that they had been unable to call witnesses because (according to the Obscene Publications Act of 1959) experts were restricted to commenting on the 'artistic merits of a work'. This aspects of the book, he insisted, was not under investigation in this particular case. He questioned whether the opinions of university lecturers and writers were those of 'ordinary men and women' who would read Penguin's cheap paperback edition. He reinforced the fact that the novel contained depictions of sexual activity that were more characteristics of the disreputable places found in most cities at home and abroad.

The Not Guilty verdict opened the way for the legal distribution of a novel that was no longer deemed to be obscene under the 1959 Act. As a result, Penguin's new edition of *Lady Chatterley's Lover* went on sale on 10 November at the price of 3s / 6d. By the end of the day, it was reported that the complete run of 200,000 copies had been sold. However, *The Times*, while acknowledging a 'great shift' in what is permissible legally, denied an equivalent transformation in popular morality. It spoke for many *'sincere people deeply concerned about public and private morals, who will be asking themselves exactly where the consequences will stop'.*

Further questions were asked about the weaknesses in the prosecution's case. In particular, why it had not been possible for the prosecution to match Penguin 'bishop for bishop, don for don' with witnesses who took the exact opposite view to those presented by the defence."
Source: *The Times*, Thursday 3 November, 1960.

On Wednesday 14 December 1960, the House of Lords debated the *Lady Chatterley* case and verdict. It was Lord Hailsham who made the concluding comments in the debate:

Viscount Hailsham's Comments

"My Lords, I end with a word to my noble friend and to other people who, like myself, share the Christian faith. It may well be that we should like to preserve the innocence of our children and society from the disasters which we believe will follow from the adoption of false creeds, false prophets and false Christs. We cannot do so by prohibiting their work by an act of law. We have to gird our loins and fight, and the battle must involve a willingness on our part, to meet our enemies in the open. To defeat them in argument, prepared to show that our beliefs are more rational than theirs. We shall not succeed in this day and

age by prohibiting their work, merely because we regard their opinions as detestable."
Source: *HANSARD*: House of Lords Debate, 14 December, 1960 Vol.227, cc 528-74].

In 1961, Penguin published a full transcript of the trial edited by CH Rolph, a former police officer turned journalist, who had previously served as secretary to the Herbert Committee in 1954. This second edition contained a dedication thanking the jurors in the trial:

> "For having published this book, Penguin Books were prosecuted under the Obscene Publications Act, 1959, at the Old Bailey in London, from 20 October to 2 November, 1960. This edition is therefore dedicated to the twelve jurors, three women and nine men who returned a verdict of Not Guilty, and this made DH Lawrence's last novel available for the first time to the public in the United Kingdom".

The trial itself became a regular source of discussion on British society during the mid-to-late 1960s. In particular, the influential testimonies of such witnesses as Bishop John Robinson and academic Richard Hoggart. What is particularly remembered is prosecutor Mervyn Griffith-Jones's misplaced question on the subject of the book's suitability for jurors' *'wives and servants'* to read.

These comments ensured that the episode was, and continues to be, regarded as more than just a literary debate on the boundaries between obscenity and decency. In many respects, it was viewed as a conflict of *'generation and class'*. However, it still remains open to discussion as to how far the verdict reached in this case, provided evidence of a significant 'shift' in public opinion.

CHAPTER THREE

The Trial In Retrospect

When Penguin Books announced it intended to publish *Lady Chatterley's Lover* uncensored in 1960, the country had to decide if Britain was ready for 'naughty words' and inter-class relationships. On the 2 November 1960, after an Old Bailey trial lasting six days, British publishers Penguin Books Limited, was found 'not guilty' under the Obscene Publications Act of 1959, for its printing of Lawrence's novel.

This landmark ruling had a significant impact on publishing and paved the way for greater publishing freedom. DH Lawrence's novel depicts an upper-class woman embarking on an affair with her working-class gamekeeper. Her aristocratic husband had been paralysed during the First World War, and this had created emotional and physical deterioration in their relationship. As well as dealing with the controversial subjects of adultery and inter-class relationships, the novel was sexually explicit, and contained words that were considered unprintable at the time. Lawrence did not live to witness the controversy his novel caused, having died in 1930.

It was not until August, 1960, that Penguin Books attempted to publish the novel in its 'unexpurgated' form. This has been considered by many as a direct challenge to the Director of Public Prosecutions, to prosecute the company for publishing an 'obscene article'. Not surprisingly, the DPP obliged. The Obscene Publications Act of 1959 prevented the publication or broadcasting of material considered to be obscene, and therefore '*likely to deprave and corrupt those exposed to it*'.

For their part, Penguin Books believed that it had a defence available to challenge the prosecution. The Act of

1959 provided such a defence, in that if a book considered obscene, could be proved to have '*literary merit*' and that its publication was in the '*public good*'. The prosecution contended that Lawrence's book did have a tendency to 'deprave' in the sense of promoting 'impure thoughts' and was likely to mitigate against the achievement of a balanced life.

Concern was raised over the social effects of its increased availability at Penguin's affordable price. Lawrence, it was argued, had failed to condemn the lovers' behaviour, the relationships were immoral, and the sexual parts of the book were inessential. The issue of marriage proved highly contentious, the prosecution underlining the novel's apparently sympathetic concentration on an adulterous affair. The prosecution relied mainly on the novel itself, its language, and the subject matter to convince the jury.

With the exception of Detective Inspector Monahan, the prosecution called no witnesses, and it cross-examined less as the trial progressed. There was a danger that the jury might well wonder why the prosecution had produced no witnesses to challenge the novel's 'literary' meaning. In addition, the prosecutions closing speech to the jury could be seen to reflect anxiety over the sheer weight of defence testimony on that subject. The defence emphasised the estimable character and behaviour of Penguin Book, along with Lawrence's standing in the world of literature. It stressed the value of making the novel available to a wider public, and Penguin Books' integrity in refusing to publish an 'expurgated' version.

The judge, Mr Justice Byrne, ruled that although the author's intention was irrelevant to the question of obscenity, it could be admissible in relation to the excusing of that obscenity on 'literary or other grounds'. The defence was organised with formidable thoroughness, and called thirty-five witnesses from a range of backgrounds; authors, academics, clergymen and teachers. Their role was to exclusively provide evidence relevant to section 4 of the Act, relating to the issue of 'literary merit' and generally they showed a high degree of consensus. Lawrence was an author of high value, but it was acknowledged that the novel was not his best, but it was certainly notable and it was in the 'public interest' that it be available.

By concentrating on the issue of 'intention', defence witnesses were able to invert the prosecution's characterisations of the novel. For example, Richard Hoggart (one of the academic witnesses) responded to examination by Mr Jeremy Hutchinson for the defence: Mr Hutchinson:*"The book has also been described as little more than vicious indulgence in sex and sensuality. In your view, is that a valid description of this novel?* Mr Hoggart: *"I think it is invalid on all three counts. It is not in any sense vicious, it is highly virtuous and if anything, puritanical."*

This view was further supported and enlarged by the writer EM Forster. When asked by Mr Hutchinson to comment on the description of Lawrence as part of the great Puritan stream of writers in his country, Forster replied:

> *"I think the description is a correct one, though I understand that first people would think it paradoxical. But when I was thinking over this matter beforehand, I considered his relationship with Bunyan. They were both preachers. They both believed intensely in what they preached. I would say, if I may speak of antecedents of great novels, Bunyan on the one hand, and Blake on the other, Lawrence too had the passionate opinion of the world, and what it ought to be, but is not".*

Further evidence from a former legislator was

offered by Norman St John Stevas. He had a unique range of qualifications; a barrister and author of the legal textbook *Obscenity and the Law.* He had drafted the original Bill which ultimately led to the passing of the Obscene Publications Act in 1959.

He was also an adviser to the Herbert Committee on the obscenity laws. St John Stevas had read a great number of books when writing *Obscenity and the Law.* He was allowed to compare those books with *Lady Chatterley's Lover,* only in respect of 'literary merit' not obscenity.

He commented:

"I have certainly read a great many books of a pornographic and obscene nature in connection with this study, and my judgement is with regard to literary merit, that of course, Lady Chatterley's Lover has nothing in common with those books. I would use 'literary merit' there not only in the sense of the language, but I do not think this can be separated from the theme and method and the underlying morality of the book. These books which I have studied have nothing to be said for them at all, and I find it difficult to make a comparison between them and Lady Chatterley's Lover, because the gulf between them is so great".

The prosecution stressed damage to society and the lack of explicit moral purpose. The defence distinguished between what was represented and the 'intention' underlying that representation. The prosecution's strategy had been to emphasise the obscenity of the novel, while rejecting the 'public good' argument. However, the weight of expert opinion produced by the defence, together with the evidence of the legislators, appears to have swayed the jury. However, there was a degree of ambiguity in the jury's verdict, for in finding Penguin Books 'not guilty' of publishing an obscene article, it failed to specify whether the novel had been found not to be obscene, or to be obscene but its publication justified in the 'public interest'.

Objections to the publication of the novel were based as much on its cheap public availability, its depiction of inter-class physical relations and its use of obscene language, as much as in its description of the sexual act itself. The novel was divisive because of its frank depictions of sex and because of the four-letter words it contained. Both would prove to be the key factors at the trial. At the time, *Lady Chatterley* became a byword for the 'risque' and scandalous but for many, the publicity which accompanied the distribution of the novel, was a watershed moment in British history, between a 'staid' Establishment-ruled past, and a more permissive future. The key factor in the decision to prosecute was that Penguin Books proposed to sell the book at 3s 6d, to put it within easy reach of women and the working-class.

With the rise in literacy rates in the early twentieth century, there was a great demand for literature, and more people were exposed to culture that had previously only been available to the elite. Allen Lane's idea for Penguin to publish 200,000 copies of *Lady Chatterley* in 1960, shows that the advent of mass culture in the early twentieth century was beginning to affect publishing in general. Education was very much a 'class indicator' in Britain at that time.

The idea that publishing had levels of elitism and segregation shows that the 1960 trial of the novel was more about the danger of the 'masses' being exposed to such radical sexual ideas, rather than what Lawrence in fact wrote. In Britain in 1960, there was a differentiation between how the upper and lower classes should behave, and what should be 'given' to them in terms of 'culture'. There is little doubt that Penguin Books wanted to tap into the lucrative opportunity presented by the rise in literacy, and the demand for cheaper books. *Lady Chatterley* was ultimately defended on its 'cultural' merit, and to the defence case that high quality fiction should be easily available to anybody that wished to read it.

The timing of the Obscene Publications Act in 1959, which replaced the 19th century law of 'obscene libel' could arguably have been the reason why Lawrence's novel was finally acquitted in court. If the defence for the novel could prove to the jury its 'literary and cultural merit', then Penguin's mass publication could only be seen as a positive step in the advancement of British culture.

Despite Lawrence's use of four-letter words throughout the novel, when viewed as a 'whole', the novel proved suitable for the public. Outlining the novel's plot, prosecutor Mervyn Griffith-Jones stated that there were twelve very detailed descriptions of sexual intercourse with the variation only being the time and place of the incidents. The emphasis was always on the pleasure, the satisfaction and the sensuality of those episodes. Mr Gerald Gardiner for the defence, submitted that the prosecution should not prejudice the jury's mind on specific passages in the novel before they had read the book as a whole, a fact specifically stated in the Act. The publishers relied on the status of Lawrence as an author and his place in English Literature. Few would disagree that he was among the six greatest English novelists of the century. The descriptions of physical union were

59

necessary to what Lawrence was trying to say, and he thought that if he used words which had been part of our spoken speech for 600 years, he could purify them from the shame which they had achieved since Victorian times.

Certain themes have been identified in the testimony of many of the defence witnesses at the time. There appears to have been an overall consensus that Lawrence was a great and gifted writer and that *Lady Chatterley* is a sincere and honest book. Far from exalting promiscuity, Lawrence regards the sexual act with a kind of reverence. The book contains many passages the witnesses described as 'poetic beauty'.

It can be seen that during the process of the trial, the prosecution resorted to a familiar technique in advocacy in dealing with the defence witnesses by urging the jury to dismiss them as lacking in 'common sense'. However, the defence anticipating this tactic, was at pains to elicit from the various witnesses testimony that they themselves had children and that they were not persons 'living a rarefied life'.

The rhetoric of the defence of *Lady Chatterley* was indignation against censorship with an appeal to enlightenment and tolerance. However, it has been suggested that R v Penguin Books may magnify the difficulty of the defence in future cases involving controversial books of some but lesser merit than *Lady Chatterley*, by authors less well known than Lawrence. This is because both judges and juries will expect a comparable procession of expert witnesses to appear.

Assuming that experts are competent, what is the permissible scope of the expert's testimony? In fact, who is an expert with respect to prevailing literary and moral community standards? In R v Penguin Books, the trial judge did make a number of important rulings concerning the allowable range of expert testimony. judge Byrne ruled that 'it is not open to the defence to call evidence to prove that there was no intention (by the author), to deprave and corrupt'. He held that while no defence could adduce evidence that publication was in the interest of learning or literature, the experts could not testify that the publication was for the 'common good'. That ultimate decision was for the jury.

A basic question which is the subject of discussion in England is whether the judicial process is appropriate for resolving issues of 'literary merit'. An assessment of a work's 'merit' involves value judgments which are far removed from judgements or questions of fact which are customarily confided to jurors. An anomaly of the Obscene Publications Act of 1959 is that it does not define 'literary merit'.

During the trial, Dr Vivian Pinto, Professor of English at Nottingham University, was asked by the defence for a definition of 'literary merit'.

Professor Pinto: *"It is not easy to put it in a few words. I look for a number of things in a book. I look for the quality of the writing, for the importance of the subject matter, the meaning of the book, whether it has a true and valid meaning. The experience that lies behind it is important and whether the artistry, the craftsmanship is adequate, and whether it succeeds in conveying the author's experience, and whether that experience is a significant experience. I think what is called the 'longimanous test' is a good test; when you come back to it, and get fresh pleasure from it, and I did just that".*

In any trial for obscenity, most juries are employed simply to decide on matters of <u>fact</u>. In other cases such as libel, they have to base their decisions on a matter of <u>opinion;</u> it is their own opinion that counts. However, in a trial for obscenity, their own opinions, in a narrow sense, may not matter.

In obscenity cases, the jury is asked to take a wide view, perhaps to set aside their own feelings that a work they may personally find revolting, is nonetheless, deemed to have 'literary or artistic' value. In such circumstances, it can be argued that public, of which the jury will, in theory, be a representative microcosm, should be encouraged to have a comprehensive idea of the book on trial, and the literary complexities surrounding it.

Was *Lady Chatterley's Lover* obscene or pornographic? Steven Marcus, in his work *The Other Victorians,* explains that one of the characteristics of pornographic prose is its constant use of cliches, expressions and stereotypes. A careful reading of the erotic passages in *Lady Chatterley* reveals a complete absence of such features. Each sentence, each word, each expression have been carefully thought out in order to express the personal, never stereotypical emotions of Lady Constance.

Connie appears as a complex character whose life appears to be operating in three stages in the novel. Firstly, as a woman full of internal conflicts who goes through a number of psychological stages regarding her relationship with Mellors, the gamekeeper. Secondly, an internal stage of emotional isolation, characterised by her struggles not to let her feelings towards him deprive her of her precious personal freedom, and finally, a last stage represented by her unconditional passion for Mellors. Another feature of pornographic language consists of parallel use of euphemisms and taboo words. Lawrence consciously avoids euphemisms. His intention is to recover those so-called obscene words so that it will be possible again to speak and think openly about sex. Lawrence certainly uses taboo words, but this does not follow a pornographic aim or displays a lack of sensibility. It results from a deep and careful reflection on the necessity to abolish once and for all, the *'secretism'* that usually surrounds sex-related issues. In Lawrence's opinion, it is precisely this 'secretism' that turns sex in pornography.

The language in *Lady Chatterley* is of an 'erotic' rather than 'pornographic' character. Evidence supporting this assertion comes from the fact that tenderness, love and other feelings are always to be found in these episodes, which have been mistakenly censored as pornographic. The novel approaches the subject of sexual relations between two adults as something natural, as a source of pleasure, not shame. It is a novel which represents the author's struggle to convey his firm conviction that a full sexual relationship cannot be detached from love, feelings and emotions.

It was Lawrence himself who explicitly defined his position towards the issue of sexual relationship in one of his letters:

> *"If there is one thing I don't like it is cheap and promiscuous sex. If there is one thing I insist on is that sex is a delicate, vulnerable, vital thing that you mustn't fool with. If there is one thing I deplore, it is heartless sex".*

[see M Squires DH Lawrence]

The language surrounding sexuality in *Lady Chatterley,* especially that of Connie is much cruder than Lawrence's previous work and offers more explicit descriptions than was generally known at the time. The sexual descriptions and connotations associated with Connie's affairs are quite explicit and Lawrence allows himself to use wording that he had not been quite so free with in the past. These descriptions and the use of explicit languages is possibly the main reasons why the novel was banned for a long time following its publication. Also, this played a part in providing Lawrence with the notoriety that has been attributed to him ever since.

However, some literary critics have suggested that the 'jump' he makes from being relatively modest in his sexual language in previous works, to the explicit language in *Lady Chatterley* may have been a premeditated change to 'provoke people and begin a controversy'.

It has also been speculated that Lawrence had thought to make a novel view sex from 'holistic' or whole perspectives, where it was physical as well as spiritual, and portrayed in a way that is full and honest.

In this sense, the novel's approach to the topic is quite successful. *Lady Chatterley's Lover* was one of the most controversial novels of the early twentieth century and was labelled as obscene by many. Those obscenities that appear in the novel are based on the fact that it tells the story of a woman who enjoys sex and finds it outside of marriage when her husband is unable to satisfy her needs.

Media Reflections On The Trial

Chatterley: When Sex Was Put On Trial

"The beginning of the Sixties saw a case which helped redefine attitudes to sex and literature. After it was over, Kenneth Tynan reflected on the jury's verdict that D H Lawrence's novel did not deprave and corrupt. Now that the case is over, and Lady Chatterley's adventures are speeding two-hundred-thousand-fold to every outpost of literacy in the country, it seems suddenly unthinkable that the jury could have brought in any other verdict. But it was desperately thinkable right up to three o'clock on Wednesday afternoon, as anyone knows who sat through the six days of trial, and sweated out the dragging hours of the jury's retirement; more than most people, Gerald Gardiner knew it, and looked the reverse of optimistic as he prowled like a wounded lion, waiting for those twelve inscrutable citizens to come to their conclusion.

How we had all stared at them, seizing on each smile, each sniffle, each sign of inattentiveness as evidence of sympathy or hostility to Lawrence's cause. The lean, middle-aged man at the right-hand end of the back row seemed prematurely grey: did this betoken sensitivity or hyper-sensitivity?

And the quietly eccentric behaviour of the woman upstage right left many of us baffled: she was given to strange, secret smiles and would take notes at inexplicable moments: an intense burst of scribbling, for instance, followed the information that one witness had been educated at Tonbridge School. In front of her sat a younger woman, sedate and pretty, perhaps a teacher; some of us pictured her as the Henry Fonda character whose gentle persistence would finally win over her colleagues, as in *Twelve Angry Men*. But against this hope, and against the waves of pro-Lawrence partisanship that flooded the court

from the public gallery, stood the unanimous opinion of the
professional crime reporters that acquittal was impossible:
'They'll never swallow those words', as one of them put it,
with a kind of cynical smugness that seems, even in
memory, peculiarly detestable. Nor, as we waited, could we
forget the summing up of the judge who, throughout the
trial, had displayed no uncontrollable impatience to get the
book into the shops. A slight, old gentleman with a mild,
dry voice, resembling beneath his robes some relict of
feudal Japan, Mr Justice Byrne could not be accused of
having loaded the dice in favour of the defence.

One remembered the tone, discreetly incredulous of
his interjections; as when he had asked Richard Hoggart to
repeat the phrase 'virtuous, if not puritanical', and had
written it down with eyebrows eloquently raised; or when
he had put to another witness the question: 'Is there really
anything else in this book except adultery?'

And his summing-up, with its reminder to the jury
that the world today seemed to be full of academic experts,
struck the same note of weary bewilderment that must have
been heard from the bench when first the psychologists and
psychiatrists strode in to the courts to confuse plain men
with their theories.

Here were professors, critics, editors and poets,
standing up in the box to deliver lectures on the nature of
literature, clouding the air with their semantic evasions,
expressing opinions instead of stating facts, and thus
dissolving the fabric of concrete truth on which the world
of law was founded when it first began. No sooner had one
witness dubbed Lawrence a puritan than another would
claim him for Catholicism, only to see someone else haul
him back, minutes later into the Protestant camp.

Nothing was simple any more; at the Old Bailey,
where matters of indecency and obscene behaviour had
traditionally been settled by policemen and doctors,
respectable men and women were talking about sex as if it

were something holy.

It must have seemed to Mr Justice Byrne that chaos was come again; no wonder he felt the need to recall the jury to sanity, to tell them that their views counted for more than those of the experts, to remind them that this was a Christian country, and to ask them rhetorically whether they perceived 'any spark of affection' between Lady Chatterley and her lover. He urged them not to get lost 'in the higher realms of literature', but to think of factory girls reading the book in their lunch-hour, a social group for whom he, like the prosecuting counsel, showed a tender recurrent regard.

This protectiveness overflowed into his exposition of the new obscenity laws. The jury had first to decide whether or not the work tended to 'deprave and corrupt': if they concluded that it did, they must go on to consider whether its publication could be justified as being 'for the public good' on the grounds of its literary and other merits. He was prompted to impress on the jury that, while the expert testimony should be given weight, the essence of the Act was contained in four words: 'for the public good'. He detached the phrase from its context, dwelling on it with affectionate iteration, so that one almost forgot that this emphasis, if heavily enough applied, would tilt the new Act towards meaningless fantasy; for a few mad moments, it seemed as if the only point at issue was whether it would be 'for the public good' to publish books that tended 'to deprave and corrupt'.

These and other passages from the summing-up haunted us and we waited. We recalled, for example, the judge's failure to mention in his survey of the defence witnesses, a name that had echoed thrillingly down the corridors of the Old Bailey on the third morning – Edward Morgan Forster, who had bowed most courteously to the bench before declaring, in prose of the greatest fastidiousness, that certainly Lawrence belonged in the puritan tradition, where his antecedents were Bunyan and Blake. We also remembered the persistence with which both judge and prosecutor had hammered it home that Lady Chatterley was an immoral woman, that she had had sexual relations before marriage, that she had committed adultery under her husband's roof; as if these charges somehow disqualified her from participation in serious literature.

Indeed, there were long periods of the trial during which an outsider might well have assumed that a divorce case was being heard; and it often seemed that the Crown was labouring under the same misapprehension, intensified by spasms of uncertainty as to whether the defendant was Constance Chatterley or Lawrence's own wife.

Over much that we heard hung the ancient fallacy that a book whose characters behave 'immorally' is therefore an immoral book; and the further fallacy that an immoral book is by definition an obscene book.

These confusions were inadvertently compounded by some of the defence witnesses, who went rather far in their eulogies of the book's ethical value; and by others who, while confining themselves to its literary merit, seemed unaware that the stress nowadays laid on the moral content of literature is something imperfectly understood by the average legal mind, to which morality means only Victorian morality.

It is significant of the modern critical climate that not once in the trial was the word 'aesthetics' mentioned. We consoled ourselves, as we kept our vigil outside the jury room, by concentrating on the good, encouraging episodes and banishing the bad ones. Apart from Mr Forster, we singled out Helen Gardner who briskly explained that since the act of sex was not shameful, neither was the word that described it; and Rebecca West, whose manner, at once firm and rambling, did not always make for good communication. We had Walter Allen and Raymond Williams, both splendidly unflappable; Stephen Potter, impressive in the unaccustomed role of Lawrence scholar; and Cecil Day Lewis, as dapper in mind as in bearing. We had the Bishop of Woolwich and the Headmaster of Alley's; from the latter pair alone, must it not have seemed to the official custodians of our morals that the whole world was ganging up on them?

And there was always, indomitable, Gerald Gardiner, that rock among silks and monument to unassertive sanity, whose final address had left no weakness in the Crown's case unexamined, from its implicit snobbishness in the matter of factory girls, to its total lack of supporting testimony. Mr Gardiner had coined phrases, too, speaking of 'a high breathlessness about beauty that cancels lust'; and he had managed to restate, without boring us, the novel's twin themes - the danger that industrialisation would destroy human relationships and the consequent need to affirm the supremacy of instinct over intellect.

Yet, had he, perhaps, presented his case with too little passion? For in all our ears there still rang the voice of Mervyn Griffith-Jones, counsel for the prosecution, high cheek-boned and poker-backed, a veteran of Eton, Trinity Hall (Cambridge), the Coldstream Guards and many previous obscenity cases; a voice passionate only in disdain, but barbed with a rabid belief in convention and discipline; a slow, scaly voice, listening to which one almost felt that if Penguin Books were acquitted, the prostitutes would dance in the streets, as they did after Oscar Wilde's conviction.

On Lawrence as a literary artist, the voice had done some dedicated homework. 'Is that expert, artistic writing?' he would ask, having cited a passage in which a phrase was several times repeated. The voice marked Lawrence as if he were an examination paper. It exhaled class consciousness as effortlessly as air. Would the jury wish their servants to read Lawrence's novel? And was it natural for the lady of a great house to, 'run off and copulate with her husband's game-keeper?'

The voice took on a positively vengeful rasp when cross-examining people who distinguished between sex, as Lawrence saw it and sex as a trivial diversion. Wasn't it true that by 'tenderness' the book actually meant tenderness towards the genital organs? And could anyone deny that in the 'bouts' of love-making the emphasis was on the 'pleasure and satisfaction' involved?

The voice hounded Connie Chatterley, a traitor to her class in that she not only enjoyed sex but enjoyed it with a quasi-peasant. A passage in which she removes her night-dress before making love, the voice enquired why this 'strip-tease' was necessary; one assumed, charitably, that the question had been carefully phrased.

Throughout the trial, one longed for a witness who might challenge Mr Griffith-Jones in Lionel Trilling's words:

> "*I see no reason in morality (or in aesthetic theory) why literature should not have as one of its intentions the arousing of thoughts of lust. It is one of the effects, perhaps one of the functions of literature to arouse desire, and I can discover no ground for saying that sexual pleasure should not be among the objects of desire which literature present to us, along with heroism, peace, death, food, wisdom, God etc*".

But nobody made that answer; and we, anxious in the corridors, had all but persuaded ourselves that no jury could withstand the impact of Mr Griffith-Jones, when the verdict was returned, and Lawrence exonerated. Looking back, I think I can isolate the crucial incident. It occurred on the third morning during the testimony of Richard Hoggart, who had called Lawrence's novel 'puritanical'. Mr Hoggart is a short, dark, young Midlands teacher of immense scholarship and fierce integrity. From the witness box he uttered a word that we had formerly heard only on the lips of Mr Griffith-Jones; he pointed out how Lawrence had striven to cleanse it of its furtive, contemptuous and expletive connotations, and use it 'in the most simple, natural way: one fucks'. There was no reaction in the court, so calmly was the word pronounced, and so literally employed. "Does it gain anything," asked Mr Gardiner, "by being printed 'f...'?" "Yes," said Mr Hoggart, "it gains a dirty suggestiveness".

Rising in cross-examination, Mr Griffith- Jones wanted to know what Mr Hoggart meant by 'puritanical', receiving an answer to the effect that a puritan was a man who felt a profound sense of responsibility to his own conscience.

Counsel then read out a series of excerpts from the novel. It must have been by chance that he chose the most impressive passages, the most solemnly ecstatic, the ones about 'the primeval roots of true beauty', and 'the sons of men and daughters of women'; but slowly as he recited them, one realised that he genuinely thought them impure and revolting. With every defiling inflection he alienated some part of the audience, seemingly unaware that what he had intended for our scorn was moving us in a way he had never foreseen; yet still he continued, bland and derisive.

Having finished, he triumphantly asked the witness whether a puritan would feel such 'reverence for a man's balls'. Indeed, yes, said Mr Hoggart almost with compassion. I remembered his earlier reply to the suggestion that Lady Chatterley's affair with Mellors was due solely to her husband's impotence. 'It is not,' he said: and in those words we heard, for the first time in the trial, the stubborn, uncompromising voice of the radical English moralist. Its volume and assurance grew as the cross-examination proceeded; and before long, both jury and audience knew that the real battle had at last be joined,

71

between all that Hoggart stood for, and all that Griffith-Jones stood for; between Lawrence's England and Sir Clifford Chatterley's England; between contact and separation, between freedom and control, between love and death".
Source: *The Guardian,* 6 November 1960,
Author: Kenneth Tynan (theguardian.com /books/1960

"Lady Chatterley Trial – 50 Years On. The Filthy Book That Set Us Free And Fettered Us Forever"

"Fifty years ago this week, amid extraordinary international publicity, the Old Bailey was the venue for a trial that did more to shape 21st-century Britain than hundreds of politicians put together. The case of the Crown versus Penguin Books opened on Friday, October 21, 1960, when courtroom officials handed copies of perhaps the most notorious novel of the century, DH Lawrence's book *Lady Chatterley's Lover*, to nine men and three women, and asked them to read it. They were not, however, allowed to take the book out of the jury room. Only if Penguin were acquitted of breaking the Obscene Publications Act would it be legal to distribute it.

What followed, said one witness, was a "circus so hilarious, fascinating, tense and satisfying, that none who sat through all its six days will ever forget them". But it was a circus that changed Britain forever. Though few then could have realised it, a tiny but unmistakable line runs from the novel Lawrence wrote in the late 1920s to an international pornography industry today worth more than £26 million a year.

Now that public obscenity has become commonplace, it is hard to recapture the atmosphere of a society that saw fit to ban books such as *Lady Chatterley's Lover* because it was likely to 'deprave and corrupt' its readers. Although only half a century separates us from Harold Macmillan's Britain, the world of 1960 can easily seem like ancient history. In a Britain when men still wore heavy grey suits, working women were still relatively rare, and the Empire was still, just a going concern, DH Lawrence's book was merely one of many banned because of its threat to public morality. Antediluvian as the early 1960s might seem to us today, however, they seemed at the same time an era of dizzying change.

73

Only a year before the trial, Roy Jenkins had secured the passage of a new Obscene Publications Act, leaving a crucial loophole - the question of literary merit - through which works might escape prohibition. And in May 1960, Penguin saw its chance, announcing its plan to publish 200,000 paperback copies at just 3s 6d, the equivalent of £3 day.

Most accounts of the trial present it as a simple clash between the repressive old Establishment on the one hand, and the youthful forces of progress and enlightenment on the other. But this is not really fair. Under Jenkin's legislation, the Crown had no choice but to prosecute: as the prosecuting counsel, Mervyn Griffith-Jones, told the director of public prosecutions: "If no action is taken in respect of this publication, it will make proceedings against any other novel very difficult".

And contrary to myth, much of the Establishment, if such a thing ever really existed, actually supported the publishers. Almost every newspaper in the country agreed that the trial was a waste of time: the Daily Telegraph thought that the police should be hunting down 'absolutely filthy' pornography rather than wasting their time with DH Lawrence.

In many respects, the celebrated landmark trial was actually something of a farce. The defence team, led by Gerald Gardiner, a founder member of CND, lined up 35 distinguished witnesses convinced of the book's literary merit, including E M Forster, Cecil Day-Lewis, Rebecca West and Richard Hoggart. The Bishop of Woolwich, John Robinson, the very prototype of a trendy Anglican clergyman, even told the court that Lawrence showed sex as 'an act of holy communion', and agreed vigorously when asked if it was a book that 'Christians ought to read'.

By contrast, the Crown was in trouble from the start. Although the prosecution drew up a long list of potential witnesses who might condemn Lawrence's book as obscene, none of them agreed to testify. At one point they even considered flying over an American literary critic who had once condemned the book as 'a dreary, sad performance with some passages of unintentional, hilarious, low comedy', although they eventually abandoned the idea.

Instead, the prosecution team wasted time before the trial going through the book line by line with a pencil, noting down the obscenities: on page 204, for example, one 'bitch goddess of Success', one 'f...ing', one 's...t', one 'best bit of c... left on earth', and three mentions of 'balls'.

Poor Mervyn Griffith-Jones, a war hero awarded the Military Cross after his service in North Africa and Italy, was totally out of his depth. It was almost in desperation that, in high-Victorian style, he asked the jury:

> "Would you approve of your young sons, young daughters-because girls can read as well as boys, reading this book? Is it a book that you would have lying around in your own house? Is it a book that you would even wish your wife or your servants to read?"

Once the words were out of his mouth, the case was lost. On November 2, after just three hours' deliberation, the jury acquitted Penguin Books of all charges. Almost immediately, the book became a best-seller. In 15 minutes, Foyles sold 300 copies and took orders for 3,000 more. Hatchards sold out in 40 minutes; Selfridges sold 250 copies in half an hour. In one Yorkshire town, a canny butcher sold copies of the book beside his lamb chops.

And yet there was another side to the story, often ignored by the history books. Outside intellectual high society, most ordinary people in 1960 remained deeply conservative, and the Home Office was flooded with letters of protest.

In Edinburgh, copies were burned on the streets, in South Wales, women librarians asked permission not to handle it; from Surrey, one anguished woman wrote to the home secretary, explaining that her teenage daughter was at a boarding school and she was terrified that 'girls there may introduce this filthy book'.

Although Philip Larkin famously wrote that sexual intercourse began *"between the end of the Chatterley ban and the Beatles' first LP"*, the truth is that Britain in the next few years remained a strikingly chaste and conservative society.

It was in the early 1970s, not the 1960s, that the sexual revolution became a reality for most people, with millions of women taking the Pill, teenagers losing their virginity earlier and divorce, homosexuality and abortion becoming familiar elements of our social landscape. In the long run, however, the end of the Chatterley ban was an enormously symbolic movement, representing the end of an era in which the state had regulated private morality as well as public behaviour.

Other obscenity cases followed in the next two decades, but they all tended to have the same result: a triumph for liberation, a defeat for censorship.

By and large, it is no exaggeration to say that after October 1960, the fetters were off.

Half a century on, the Lady Chatterley trial has become a cliché of the conventional Sixties narrative, a victory for youth and freedom against a repressive old order. But in a society where pre-pubescent girls stroll down the high street wearing T-shirts with the legend "Porn star", I wonder whether its legacy is more double-edged. Britain in 2010 is unquestionably a much more open society; most of us would think it intolerable to return to a time when the state regulated what we could and could not write. Few of us, I suspect, would wish that the verdict in the Chatterley case had gone differently.

Yet will future generations judge that we used our freedom wisely? I doubt it. As the frescoes at Pompeii remind us, erotica and pornography have been elements of almost every society since the dawn of civilisation. But you do not have to be Mary Whitehouse to question the way pornography has filtered into our cultural mainstream, or to feel uneasy about the way very young girls are portrayed as willing and available sex objects. Kicking against their elders, the reformers of the Sixties worshipped freedom and self-expression; as they saw it, discipline and self-restraint had manifestly gone too far.

But 50 years on from the trial that changed Britain forever, living in a society where the bonds of community and courtesy have frayed almost beyond repair, we could surely do with rather more of Mervyn Griffith-Jones's much-mocked puritanism. We might not be able to turn the clock back. But it is never too late to learn from the past". Source: *The Daily Telegraph* 16 October, 2010 Author: Dominic Sandbrook (telegraph.co.uk/culture/books/Lady Chatterley Trial.

"The Trial Of Lady Chatterley's Lover"

"The Old Bailey has, for centuries, provided the ultimate arena for challenging the state. But of all its trials, for murder or mayhem, for treason and sedition-none has had such profound and political consequences as the trial in 1960 of Penguin Book for publishing *Lady Chatterley's Lover.* The verdict was a crucial step towards the freedom of the written word, at least for works of literary merit (works of no literary merit were not safe until the trial of Oz in 1971, and works of demerit had to await the acquittal of *Inside Linda Lovelace* in 1977). But the *Chatterley* trial marked the first symbolic moral battle between the humanitarian force of English liberalism and the dead hand of those described by George Orwell as "the striped-trousered ones who rule", a battle joined in the 1960s on issues crucial to human rights, including the legalisation of homosexuality and abortion, abolition of the death penalty and of theatre censorship, and reform of the divorce laws. The acquittal of *Lady Chatterley* was the first sign that victory was achievable, and with the guidance of the book's great defender, Gerald Gardiner QC (Labour Lord Chancellor 1964-70), victory was, in due course, achieved.

There is a myth that freedom of speech has been safely protected in England by the jury. This is almost precisely the opposite of the truth. Old Bailey juries (comprised until 1972 solely of property owners) usually did what they were told by judges, and convicted. Until 1959, the publisher of a book that contained any "purple pages" that might have a "tendency to deprave and corrupt those whose minds are open to such immoral influences" was liable to imprisonment. Literary standards were set at what was deemed acceptable reading for 14-year-old schoolgirls - whether or not they could, or would want to, read it. Merit was no defence: in 1928 Radcliffe Hall's *The Well of Loneliness* was destroyed by a magistrate who

78

realised to his horror that one line in the novel ("and that night they were not divided") meant that two female characters had been to bed together. He said this would "induce thoughts of a most impure character and would glorify the horrible tendency of lesbianism"; the prosecution had Rudyard Kipling attend the court, in case the magistrate needed a literary expert to persuade him to "keep the Empire pure".

Censorship of sexual references in literature was pervasive in England in the 1930s (there was a brief respite for James Joyce's *Ulysses* when a sumptuously bound copy was found among the papers of a deceased lord chancellor). In the 1950s police seized copies of the Kinsey report and prosecuted four major publishers for works of modern fiction - three were convicted.

In this period, books by Henry Miller, Lawrence Durrell, Cyril Connolly and others were available only to those English readers who could afford to travel to Paris to purchase them. In 1959, persuaded by the Society of Authors, parliament passed a new Obscene Publications Act with a preamble that promised "to provide for the protection of literature and to strengthen the law against pornography".

The distinction was to prove elusive, certainly to the attorney general, Reginald Manningham-Buller. In August 1960 he read the first four chapters of *Lady Chatterley's Lover* on the boat train to Southampton and wrote to the director of public prosecutions approving the prosecution of Penguin Books ("I hope you get a conviction"). The key factor in the decision to prosecute was that Penguin proposed to sell the book for 3/6; in other words, to put it within easy reach of women and the working classes. This, the DPP's files reveal, was what upper-middle-class male lawyers and politicians of the time refused to tolerate.

The choice of *Lady Chatterley* as a test-case was inept, but it suited the anti-intellectual temper of the legal establishment, and it would mean the defeat of an impeccably liberal cause. Besides, D H Lawrence had form. Back in 1915 all copies of *The Rainbow* had been seized by police and burned (as much for its anti-war message as for its openness about sex).

In 1928, police threatened the publisher Martin Secker with prosecution unless it removed 13 pages from *Pansies,* a book of Lawrence's poems. The publisher complied, but it sent all its unexpurgated copies abroad. The following year police raided an exhibition of Lawrence's painting and seized every canvas on which they could identify any wisp of pubic hair.

For the next 30 years, British customs erected a *cordon sanitaire* to keep out smuggled copies of *Lady Chatterley,* which by this time was being published in France and Italy. So Lawrence was entrenched in prudish English minds as the filthy fifth columnist, an enemy much more dangerous than predictably filthy foreigners such as De Sade or Nabokov. With parochial arrogance, the prosecuting authorities ignored the New York court of appeal, which in 1959 had overturned a ban on *Lady Chatterley* because it was written with "a power and tenderness which was compelling" and which justified its use of four-letter Anglo-Saxon words. Those words were a red rag to Manningham-Buller and the "grey elderly ones" (as Lawrence had described his censors), a breach of the etiquette and decorum relied on to cover up unpleasant truths.

In 1960, in the interests of keeping wives dutiful and servants touching their forelocks, Lady Constance Chatterley's affair with a gamekeeper was unmentionable.

The prosecutors were complacent: they would have the judge on their side, and a jury comprised of people of property, predominantly male, middle-aged, middle-minded and middle-class. And they had four-letter words galore: the prosecuting counsel's first request was that a clerk in the DPP's office should count them carefully. In his opening speech to the jury, he played them as if they were trump cards: "The word 'fuck' or 'fucking' appears no less than 30 times... 'Cunt' 14 times; 'balls' 13 times; 'shit' and 'arse' six times apiece; 'cock' four times; 'piss' three times, and so on".

But what the prosecution failed to comprehend was that the 1959 Act had wrought some important changes in the law. Although it retained a "tendency to deprave and corrupt" as the test for obscenity, books had now to be "taken as a whole", that is, not judged solely on their purple passage, and only in respect of persons likely to read them; in other words, not 14-year-old schoolgirls, unless they were directed to that teenage market.

Most importantly, section 4 of the Act provided that even if the jury found that the book tended to deprave and corrupt, it could nonetheless acquit if persuaded that publication "is justified in the interests of science, literature, art and learning or any other object of general concern".

The unsung hero of the trial, Penguin's solicitor, Michael Rubinstein, threw himself into the task of recruiting expert witnesses for the defence - not just professors of literature but famous novelists and unknown novelists, journalists, psychologists and even clerics.

After the case had been lost, the attorney general pretended that the Crown had disdained to match the defence "bishop for bishop and don for don", but this was a lie. In fact, the prosecution made desperate attempts to find anyone of distinction who might support a ban on Lawrence's novel.

The DPP's first suggestion was to rely again on Kipling until it was discovered that he had died in 1936. TS Eliot turned them down, as did FR Leavis (although he also refused to testify for the defence) and Helen Gardner, reader in English literature at Oxford, who told the DPP (as she was later to tell the jury) that the book was the work of a writer of genius and complete integrity. It is a measure of the narrowness of legal education in England in those days that this has simply not occurred to the lawyers in the DPP's office or to the team of Treasury Counsel, a pampered, old Etonian set of barristers who conduct major prosecutions at the Old Bailey before their inevitable elevation to its judicial benches.

Its leader, Mervyn Griffith-Jones, had no interest in literature: he was the incarnation of upper-middle-class morality, obsessed with the book's danger to social order. His famously asinine question about wives and servants was asked rhetorically and with utter sincerity.

Griffith-Jones's assumptions about society reflected his station in it, and as the trial developed, he seemed more scandalised by adultery - especially with a servant - than by the four-letter words that had preoccupied him at the start. Those few witnesses he bothered to cross-examine were tackled on subjects he knew nothing about, and he tried to cover up his own confusion with gratuitous insults ("you are not at Leicester University at the moment").

Ignorant of the facts as well as the facts of life, Griffith-Jones failed even to recognise Lawrence's paean to anal sex. ("Not very easy, sometimes, not very easy, you know to know what in fact he is driving at in that passage"). After the trial the warden of All Souls, John Sparrow, wrote an article in Encounter claiming that the jury would have convicted had the prosecution been able to identify which passage was being driven at, but he, too, did not understand the new law.

Under the 1959 Act, purple passage, even on the subject of heterosexual buggery (still the "abominable crime"), no longer necessarily meant a guilty verdict. Jurors had to ask themselves the common-sense question of whether the publication as a whole would do any harm and, if so, whether its literary merit might redeem it.

82

The tactical superiority of the defence team was evident from the outset. In a daring move on the first day of the trial, Gardiner and Jeremy Hutchinson QC declined the judge's invitation to invoke the sexist law that allowed them to empanel an all-male jury in obscenity cases, and even used their right of challenge to add a third female juror. They realised the danger that an all-male jury might be over-protective towards women in their absence, and they calculated that the prosecution's paternalism would alienate female jurors. Gardiner's forensic performance, transcribed in C H Rolph's Penguin Special *The Trial of Lady Chatterley,* was a masterclass in modern barristering. He eschewed the histrionics of Old Bailey hacks like Marshall Hall ("look at her, gentlemen of the jury. God never gave her a chance - won't you?"). Instead, he addressed the jury in powerful but straightforward language, respecting them but never condescending or playing obviously to their sympathy. He firmly indicated that they, not the judge, were responsible for the verdict. Had there been no jury, Justice Byrne would certainly have convicted. Byrne directed the jury to consider whether the book "portrays the life of an immoral woman", to remember the meaning of "lawful marriage" in a Christian country and to reflect that "the gamekeeper, incidentally, had a wife also. Thus what the ultimate result there would be is a matter for you to consider".

judges in 1960 regarded themselves, rather more than they do today, as the custodians of moral virtue. In performing this egregious function, they came to blur the distinction between literature and life. Their confusion was well represented by Lord Hailsham, in the parliamentary debate that followed the verdict:

"Before I accepted as valid or valuable or even excusable the relationship between Lady Chatterley and Mellors, I should have liked to know what sort of parents they became to the

83

child. I should have liked to see the kind of house they proposed to set up together; I should have liked to know how Mellors would have survived living on Connie's rentier income of £600. and I should have liked to know whether they acquired a circle of friends, or if not, how their relationship survived social isolation".

So far as Byrne and Griffith-Jones were concerned, the function of the modern novel was that laid down by Oscar Wilde's Miss Prism: "the good end happily, the bad end unhappily - that is what 'fiction' means". The acquittal was a victory for moral relativism and sexual tolerance, as well as for literary freedom.

No other jury verdict in British history has had such a deep social impact. Over the next three months, Penguin sold 3 m copies of the book - an example of what many years later was described as *"the Spycatcher effect"*, by which the attempt to suppress a book through unsuccessful litigation serves only to promote huge sales. The jury - that iconic representative of democratic society - had given its imprimatur to ending the taboo on sexual discussion in art and entertainment. Within a few years, the stifling censorship of the theatre by the lord chamberlain had been abolished, and a gritty realism emerged in British cinema and drama. (*Saturday Night and Sunday Morning* came out at the same time as the unexpurgated *Lady Chatterley,* and very soon Peter Finch was commenting on Glenda Jackson's "tired old tits" in *Sunday Bloody Sunday,* and Ken Tynan said the first "fuck" on the BBC).

Homosexuality was decriminalised, abortions were available on reasonable demand, and in order to obtain a divorce, it was unnecessary to prove that a spouse had committed the "matrimonial crime" of adultery. judges no longer put on black caps to sentence prisoners to hang by the neck until dead. In 1960, Sir Allen Lane took some risks and suffered a lot of personal abuse, although his lawyers adroitly arranged for the case to be brought against the company rather than its directors in person, so there was never any danger of a prison sentence.

But he put his company in peril for a principle: "My idea was to produce a book that would sell at the price of 10 cigarettes". Books have increased in price even more than cigarettes over the past 50 years and caused a lot more harm. Indeed, the message of *Lady Chatterley's Lover*, half a century after the trial, is that literature in itself does no harm at all. The damage that gets attributed to books is caused by the actions of people who try to suppress them".

The Guardian, 22 October, 2010: Author - Geoffrey Robertson QC (theguardian.com/books/2010)

"How Huge Gamble By 'Lady Chatterley' Lawyers Changed Obscenity Law Forever"

"Penguin's decision to publish 200,000 copies of *Lady Chatterley's Lover* on the advice of Jeremy Hutchinson and lead defence counsel Gerald Gardiner, was a massive gamble. It set up a case that were it not for the incompetence of the prosecution, could easily have gone the other way. *'Lady Chatterley's Lover'* had only ever legally been published in abridged versions in the UK starting in 1932. Though by 1960, the unexpurgated edition was sold in Europe and America, and could be obtained 'under the counter' in London. Penguin's co-founder Allen Lane, wanted to publish a cheap paperback of the full version. The idea was to put it out at 3s 6d, the same price as 10 cigarettes, to make it affordable for the 'young and hoi polloi'.

The excuse was the 30th anniversary of Lawrence's death from TB at the age of 45. When Penguin consulted Hutchinson and Gardiner, the lawyers retreated to reflect. A trial under the new Obscene Publications Act seemed inevitable. After a consultation with several literary experts, Hutchinson and Gardiner felt most of the racy scenes and bad language could fall under the defence that they were 'in the interests of science, literature etc'.

However, Hutchinson was concerned about page 258 of the novel, where anal sex crops up, albeit obliquely. While homosexual anal sex between consenting men was legalised in 1967 in the UK, the heterosexual equivalent became legal only in 2000 in England and Wales, and was certainly highly illegal in 1960.

However, illegal acts could still potentially use the 'public good' defence, but Hutchinson feared it made the case much harder to win. Gardiner and the experts at the meeting dismissed his fears. In these more innocent times, they were betting that the prosecution wouldn't grasp the point, and omit it from their case. Hutchinson agreed to go ahead, and advised Penguin accordingly. The defence called 35 professors of literature, authors, journalists, editors, publishers and four Anglican churchmen. Each declared the book had sufficient 'literary merit' to deserve publication, 'for the public good'.

Lead prosecutor Mervyn Griffith-Jones cross-examined only 14 of the 35. He lost most of those rounds and sometimes his temper in the process. It was only in his closing speech he said to the jury: "Would you look at page 258. It is a passage which I have not, and I do not think that anybody has, referred to during the course of cross-examination or indeed at any time during this trial. It describes what is called the 'night of sensual pleasure'. He read out the whole passage remarking: 'It is not very easy, sometimes not very easy to know what in fact he is driving at in that passage'".

It is not clear how many jurors understood the passage. Some were said to be visibly shocked. Certainly Griffith-Jones had missed the significance entirely, having referred to it only to understand the book's general depravity. Mr Justice Byrne summed-up with no reference to anal sex either. The jury returned in three hours and found Penguin not guilty. Neither the clergy, nor any of the other experts had been examined on anal sex, and it is not clear whether they realised they were implicitly defending it, or not.

A watershed in British obscenity law had been achieved without any discussion about the 'illegal' sex acts central to the novel. In the wake of this case, publishing in Britain became considerably more liberal. Had Hutchinson not agreed to advise Penguin to take that extraordinary guidance, this could have panned out very differently." Source: *The Independent,* 21 November, 2017. Author: Sue Rabbitt Roff, Tutor in Medical Education, University of Dundee.

Censorship, Saucy Readers And Sex With Lady Chatterley

"There is no reason to ban a book, if a book spreads or incites hatred, then put a warning on the cover. *'Lady Chatterley's Lover'* does not meet these criteria, yet, it was heavily censored in Britain for over 30 years. The novel had the authorities worried that it would undermine the fabric of society. It is not a book on terrorism or assassination, it is about explicit extra-marital sex.

The Establishment were terrified of *Lady Chatterley's Lover*. The prosecution asked the jury; "Is this a book you would want your wife or servant to read?" These questions reeks of patriarchal anxiety. It assumes the inferiority of women and the working-classes. It confuses social vulnerability with mental weakness. It implies that these groups should not read Lawrence's book, because they will get ideas above their station. The mid-century Establishment were worried that the narratives of adulterous sexuality would 'deprave and corrupt'.

However, if the Establishment were worried that subversive texts heralded movements towards liberation and freedom, they were right. Regardless of whether *'Lady Chatterleys Lover'* deserved to be banned, its banning was inevitable. It was predictable, so if Lawrence knew the book would be banned, why write it? There are many schools of thought on this question, but most obviously, sex is interesting, it is an entertaining topic, so why not? Unless it is banned, sex sells, and often banning it, makes it sell more.

Lawrence's work shows a passion for realistic representations of life in its narrative and its dialogue. Lawrence had a working-class background and *'Lady Chatterley's Lover'* includes working-class voices and struggles. The sex in *Lady Chatterley's Lover* is explicit, but it is not particularly sexy. It is intimate and comic. As sex is such a diverse and unique practice, it brings a challenge to deciding whether sex in stories is realism or erotica. The book, to many, is about freedom. The importance of texts like Lawrence's was to bring sex out of the Victorian euphemism and, boldly into the mainstream. It opens people's minds to the success of artistic-open-mindedness.

The purpose of *'Lady Chatterley's Lover'* was honesty and exploration. Ultimately, working-class accents occur in Britain, so an accurate presentation of British life should include them. Not only do people f..., but they also use the word f.....g. This word had a special focus in the 1960 trial, the prosecution noted that these words occurred no fewer than thirty times. The prosecution tried to determine by the numbers, whether it was art or obscenity. The novel is not pornography, but if it is, it is authentic. It strives for the real, whereas pornography exaggerates and alters reality. Lawrence's work shows a passion for realistic representation of life in its narrative and its dialogue." Source: *Expose:* The University of Exeter Independent Student Newspaper, 14 December, 2018. Author: Zach Mayford.

"The Book That Changed Britain: Why The 'Lady Chatterley's Lover' Trial Still Matters 60 Years Later"

"The trial was a contest between the future and stasis. Actually the Obscene Publications Act in fact was a liberalisation of the law, previously there had been no defence for literary merit, and it was still out of date as soon as it was enacted. The trial represented the blunt force of the law used to attempt to slow social change. It was a tactic with a long record of failure, as we still see in government responses to political protests. Perhaps the best symbol of how the *'Lady Chatterley's Lover'* trial

continues to embody change in brought about is that last
year, the copy of the book annotated by Mr Justice Byrne
was sold for more than £50,000 to an overseas bidder.
Immediately, the UK's arts minister put a hold on the book
leaving the UK. So a crowdfunding effort took place to
keep this 'important part of our nation's heritage' in the
country. As a result, the judge's copy was acquired by
Bristol University, and a book which began as a scourge of
the establishment had become in the end, a token of
national pride."
Source: penguin.co.uk /articles/2020: Author: John Self, 20
October, 2020.

The literary expert Richard Hoggart, one of the defence
witnesses at the trial wrote in his autobiography of the trial:
*"It has been entered on the agreement list of literary
judgements, as the moment at which the confused mesh of
British attitudes to class, to literature, to the intellectual
life, and to censorship, clashed as rarely before, to the
confession of more conservative attitudes"*.
("A Measured Life" page 52).

The trial of R v Penguin Books Limited attracted
widespread interest both at home and abroad, to become
one of the best known episodes in modern British legal
history. More widely as the result of social commentators,
creative writers and historians, the trial has been cast as the
catalyst for the changing of post-war attitudes towards
social order and public decency. It has also been viewed as
the starting point for a decade of conflict between the
championing moralism and liberalism.

Lady Chatterley had been considered obscene for
more than thirty years, and was finally firmly believed to
be *'an honest, healthy book, necessary for us today'*. The
case demonstrated the changes in society in tolerating the
representation of sex and sexual relations in literature.

One of the prominent considerations in the trial of 'Lady Chatterley' was its 'literary merit'. *The New York Times* in its editorial on 16 June, 1959 remarked: *"Whatever one thinks of the DH Lawrence novel, and the critics on the whole think well of it, it is a serious, literary work, with an established reputation".*

The novel demonstrates how the First World War changed English society and the individual. Lawrence, who was a strong opponent of the war, describes the negative effects of it. He leaves the reader with a 'hope' note, ending the novel with the fulfilling relationship between the protagonists Connie and Mellors. The emotional journey from a shattered society, to a life-affording one is the central theme of the novel. *Lady Chatterley's Lover* embodies Lawrence's belief in the necessity of men and women in overcoming the restrictions of industrialised society, and following the natural instincts to passionate love. It may have taken thirty years for people to understand this perspective, yet the change of perspectives on obscenity does occur. The trial eased the freedom of literary works against the threat of censorship of obscenity, as long as the work proves to have 'literary merit'.

The trial also led to a more liberal interpretation of obscenity. *Lady Chatterley's Lover* was finally able to regain its position in the literary world. Michael Squires in his work *"The Creation of Lady Chatterley's Lover"* admirably summarises the legacy of the novel: *"From tainted, smuggled, underground novel, to a work of art, whose status is widely recognised, and whose beauties are newly discovered by readers every year".* ['The Creation of Lady Chatterley's Lover, page 202].

APPENDIX

Obscene Publications Act, 1959
7 & 8 ELIZ. 2   CH. 66

ARRANGEMENT OF SECTIONS

LONDON: PUBLISHED BY HER MAJESTY'S STATIONERY OFFICE
8d. net

CHAPTER 66

An Act to amend the law relating to the publication of
obscene matter; to provide for the protection of
literature; and to strengthen the law concerning
pornography.   [29th July, 1959]

BE it enacted by the Queen's most Excellent Majesty, by and
with the advice and consent of the Lords Spiritual and
Temporal, and Commons, in this present Parliament
assembled, and by the authority of the same, as follows:—

1.—(1) For the purposes of this Act an article shall be deemed Test of
to be obscene if its effect or (where the article comprises two or obscenity.
more distinct items) the effect of any one of its items is, if taken
as a whole, such as to tend to deprave and corrupt persons who are
likely, having regard to all relevant circumstances, to read, see
or hear the matter contained or embodied in it.

(2) In this Act "article" means any description of article
containing or embodying matter to be read or looked at or both,
any sound record, and any film or other record of a picture or
pictures.

(3) For the purposes of this Act a person publishes an article
who—

  (*a*) distributes, circulates, sells, lets on hire, gives, or lends
     it, or who offers it for sale or for letting on hire; or

  (*b*) in the case of an article containing or embodying matter
     to be looked at or a record, shows, plays or projects it:

A 2   1

15 & 16 Geo.
6 & 1 Eliz. 2.
c. 68.
9 Edw. 7.
c. 30.

Provided that paragraph (*b*) of this subsection shall not apply to anything done in the course of a cinematograph exhibition (within the meaning of the Cinematograph Act, 1952), other than one excluded from the Cinematograph Act, 1909, by subsection (4) of section seven of that Act (which relates to exhibitions in private houses to which the public are not admitted), or to anything done in the course of television or sound broadcasting.

Prohibition of
publication of
obscene
matter.

2.—(1) Subject as hereinafter provided, any person who, whether for gain or not, publishes an obscene article shall be liable—

> (*a*) on summary conviction to a fine not exceeding one hundred pounds or to imprisonment for a term not exceeding six months;

> (*b*) on conviction on indictment to a fine or to imprisonment for a term not exceeding three years or both.

(2) Notwithstanding anything in section one hundred and four of the Magistrates' Courts Act, 1952, summary proceedings for an offence against this section may be brought at any time within twelve months from the commission of the offence; and paragraph 16 of the First Schedule to the Magistrates' Courts Act, 1952 (under which an offence at common law of publishing, exhibiting or selling obscene articles may be tried summarily) is hereby repealed.

15 & 16 Geo. 6
& 1 Eliz 2. c.
55.

(3) A prosecution on indictment for an offence against this section shall not be commenced more than two years after the commission of the offence.

(4) A person publishing an article shall not be proceeded against for an offence at common law consisting of the publication of any matter contained or embodied in the article where it is of the essence of the offence that the matter is obscene.

(5) A person shall not be convicted of an offence against this section if he proves that he had not examined the article in respect of which he is charged and had no reasonable cause to suspect that it was such that his publication of it would make him liable to be convicted of an offence against this section.

(6) In any proceedings against a person under this section the question whether an article is obscene shall be determined without regard to any publication by another person unless it could reasonably have been expected that the publication by the other person would follow from publication by the person charged.

Powers of
search and
seizure.

3.—(1) If a justice of the peace is satisfied by information on oath that there is reasonable ground for suspecting that, in any premises in the petty sessions area for which he acts, or on any stall or vehicle in that area, being premises or a stall or vehicle

2

specified in the information, obscene articles are, or are from time to time, kept for publication for gain, the justice may issue a warrant under his hand empowering any constable to enter (if need be by force) and search the premises, or to search the stall or vehicle, within fourteen days from the date of the warrant, and to seize and remove any articles found therein or thereon which the constable has reason to believe to be obscene articles and to be kept for publication for gain.

(2) A warrant under the foregoing subsection shall, if any obscene articles are seized under the warrant, also empower the seizure and removal of any documents found in the premises or, as the case may be, on the stall or vehicle which relate to a trade or business carried on at the premises or from the stall or vehicle.

(3) Any articles seized under subsection (1) of this section shall be brought before a justice of the peace acting for the same petty sessions area as the justice who issued the warrant, and the justice before whom the articles are brought may thereupon issue a summons to the occupier of the premises or, as the case may be, the user of the stall or vehicle to appear on a day specified in the summons before a magistrates' court for that petty sessions area to show cause why the articles or any of them should not be forfeited; and if the court is satisfied, as respects any of the articles, that at the time when they were seized they were obscene articles kept for publication for gain, the court shall order those articles to be forfeited:

Provided that if the person summoned does not appear, the court shall not make an order unless service of the summons is proved.

(4) In addition to the person summoned, any other person being the owner, author or maker of any of the articles brought before the court, or any other person through whose hands they had passed before being seized, shall be entitled to appear before the court on the day specified in the summons to show cause why they should not be forfeited.

(5) Where an order is made under this section for the forfeiture of any articles, any person who appeared, or was entitled to appear, to show cause against the making of the order may appeal to quarter sessions; and no such order shall take effect until the expiration of fourteen days after the day on which the order is made, or, if before the expiration thereof notice of appeal is duly given or application is made for the statement of a case for the opinion of the High Court, until the final determination or abandonment of the proceedings on the appeal or case.

(6) If as respects any articles brought before it the court does not order forfeiture, the court may if it thinks fit order the person on whose information the warrant for the seizure of the articles

was issued to pay such costs as the court thinks reasonable to any person who has appeared before the court to show cause why those articles should not be forfeited; and costs ordered to be paid under this subsection shall be enforceable as a civil debt.

(7) For the purposes of this section the question whether an article is obscene shall be determined on the assumption that copies of it would be published in any manner likely having regard to the circumstances in which it was found, but in no other manner.

20 & 21 Vict.
c. 83.

(8) The Obscene Publications Act, 1857, is hereby repealed, without prejudice, however, to the execution of any warrant issued thereunder before the commencement of this Act or to the taking of any proceedings in pursuance of a warrant so issued.

Defence of
public good.

4.—(1) A person shall not be convicted of an offence against section two of this Act, and an order for forfeiture shall not be made under the foregoing section, if it is proved that publication of the article in question is justified as being for the public good on the ground that it is in the interests of science, literature, art or learning, or of other objects of general concern.

(2) It is hereby declared that the opinion of experts as to the literary, artistic, scientific or other merits of an article may be admitted in any proceedings under this Act either to establish or to negative the said ground.

Citation, com-
mencement and
extent.

5.—(1) This Act may be cited as the Obscene Publications Act, 1959.

(2) This Act shall come into operation on the expiration of one month beginning with the date of the passing thereof.

(3) This Act shall not extend to Scotland or to Northern Ireland.

Produced in the U.K. for
W.J. SHARP
Controller and Chief Executive of Her Majesty's Stationery Office
and Queen's Printer of Acts of Parliament
LONDON: PUBLISHED BY HER MAJESTY'S STATIONERY OFFICE

.ʜ . 35 .

PRINTED IN ENGLAND BY SWIFT (PRINTING & DUPLICATING), LTD., FOR
C. H. BAYLIS
Controller of Her Majesty's Stationery Office and Queen's Printer of Acts of Parliament
LONDON: PUBLISHED BY HER MAJESTY'S STATIONERY OFFICE

net

4

SELECTED BIBLIOGRAPHY

Bedford, S. *The Trial of Lady Chatterley's Lover* (Daunt Books, London, 2016).

Blom-Cooper, L & Drewry, G. *Law and Morality* (Duckworth, London, 1976).

Chandos, J (ed) *To Deprave and Corrupt: Original Studies in the Nature and Definition of Obscenity* (Souvenir Press, London, 1962).

Craig, A. *Suppressed Books: A History of the Conception of Literary Obscenity* (Cleveland & New York, The World Publishing Company, 1963).

Hodgson, N. "Obscenity Trial Shows Up Outdated Law" (Law Society Gazette, London, 9 January, 2012).

Hoggart, R. *A Measured Life: The Times and Places of an Orphaned Intellectual*, (Routledge London, 1994).

Huston, T. *Reader's Guide to Great Twentieth-Century English Novels* (London, 1973).

Hyde, H.M. *The Lady Chatterley's Lover Trial* (Bodley Head, London, 1990).

Hyder, C.K. (ed) *Swinburne: The Critical Heritage* (Routledge Kegan Paul, London,1970).

Lewis, J. *Penguin Special: The Life and Times of Allen Lane* (Harmondsworth, Penguin Books, 2005).

Lockhart, W.B. & McClure, R.C. *Why Obscene: To Deprave and Corrupt: Original Studies in the Nature and Definition of Obscenity* (Souvenir Press, London, 1962).

Marcus, S. *The Other Victorians: A Study of Sexuality and Pornography in Mid- Nineteenth-Century England* (Besic Books, New York, 1964).

Rolph, C.H. (ed) *The Trial of Lady Chatterley: Regina v Penguin*

97

Books Limited (Harmondsworth, Penguin Books, 1961).

Roodhouse, M. "Lady Chatterley and the Monk: Anglican Radicals and the Lady Chatterley Trial of 1960", *Journal of Ecclesiastical History* (59, 2008, 475 – 500).

Squires, M. D.H. Lawrence: Lady Chatterley's Lover and A Propos of Lady Chatterley's Lover (Cambridge University Press, 2002).

Squires, M. The Creation of Lady Chatterley's Lover, (Baltimore & London, The John Hopkins University Press, 1983).

St. John Stevas, N. *Obscenity and the Law* (Secker and Warburg, London, 1956).

Williams, R. *Culture and Society*, 1780-1950,(Harmondsworth, Penguin Books, 1958-1961).

Yates, N. *Love Now, Pay Later: Sex and Religion in the Fifties and Sixties* (SPCK, London, 2011).

Criminal Law Review: 176, (1961).

The "Lady Chatterley's Lover Case: HANSARD: Parliamentary Debates, 227. House of Lords, 14 December, 1960, col 528-574.

The Queen v Penguin Books: "Lady Chatterleys Lover by D,H, Lawrence": Prosecution for Obscenity: National Archives, 1960-61 – LO /2/ 148.

Obscene Publications Bill (Second Reading) HANSARD: Parliamentary Debates, 546, House of Commons, 25 November, 1955, col 1883-1892.

The "Lady Chatterley Trial" - Archive Papers, D.M. 1679. University of Bristol Library.

R v Hicklin, Law Review 3, QB, 360.

Printed in Great Britain
by Amazon

26762311R00056